Lessons Learned?
Reflecting on forty years in child care.

A Memoir by John Fitzgerald

Editor Philippa May

First published 2018
by Rowanvale Books Ltd
The Gate
Keppoch Street
Roath
Cardiff
CF24 3JW
www.rowanvalebooks.com

A CIP catalogue record for this book is available from the British Library.
ISBN: 978-1-911569-99-2

Contents

Dedication

This book is dedicated to the countless numbers of children and young people with whom I and colleagues became involved during my professional career to try to disentangle damaged lives and others, for whom, sadly, it was too late, having been killed by carers or strangers. I always felt I learnt and gained more from them than I was ever able to give in return.

Acknowledgements

1. My parents, who gave me the kind of love and support every child needs, but also showed me how to have an open view of the world.

2. My two grown-up children, Mairion and Alun, whose childhood included living with a less than perfect father. My professional life meant they too were exposed at times to information that would not necessarily be available in most homes and would mean I was not always easily accessible. My thanks to them that, even today, they do not hold those imperfections against me.

3. To my wife Liz who, over the last sixteen years, has not only had to cope with living with me as I turned into a grumpy old man, but still

managed to bring a special happiness into the latter years of my life whilst taking on the task of correcting my spelling and/or grammar!

4.   To my former partner Jenny who had to live through some of my darkest days as an adult, both professionally and personally, and who helped me cope with the stress of some of the biggest child death cases in the UK.

5.   To my amazing editor Philippa May who somehow has taken my incoherent ramblings and shaped them into a book that is almost readable.

6.   To Joyce Brand and Mhairi Black who read the final draft and provided objective and invaluable comments.

7.   To the very many people (too many to list) who have played a significant part in the development of my life both professionally and personally and contributed so much to what and who I am.

8.   All royalties from the sale of this book to be donated to Glasbury Arts.

Introduction

The social work profession is singularly lacking in heroic role models. John Fitzgerald in his memoir goes a long way to putting this to right. Lessons Learned? is not only an account of a life well lived but a hymn to the very special nature of social work with abused children. Reading of his experiences in growing up in a working-class family in post-war Britain is to be reminded that the gap between the affluent and the rest is no new phenomenon, but it is also a reminder that opportunities to pursue a professional life of value were a possibility for working class children in a way that has all but disappeared.

However, it is the inspirational account of his working life in the field of child care and, in particular, child protection that makes his book essential reading for anyone wanting to understand and support investment in preventative and safeguarding work with children and families. The poignant vignettes of children's ruined lives do not make easy reading, but they do illustrate the requirement that social workers intervening in those lives do so on the basis of a sound body of knowledge with essential humanity. John demonstrates the importance of vigour in the work but not at the expense of empathy. Had I any influence on social work training I would make his book required course reading.

Joyce Brand
**Former Assistant Director (AD) Social Services in a
London Borough.**

Prologue

*"Art washes away from the soul the dust
of everyday life"*
Picasso

I spent my entire professional life working in the arena of child care, the final 20 years working on inquiries and investigations into the deaths of children through abuse. Among those investigations were high profile cases including murders of children, young people and young women carried out by Fred and Rosemary West, plus continual instances of the most horrific sexual abuse, torture and trafficking.

Over the last 30 years, faced with these unimaginable incidents, public agencies and governments have repeatedly vowed that "lessons will be learned", but have they been? How did I and others do in our world and what part did politics play? And to what extent did my own childhood experiences lead me to follow this path?

A working life which involves exposure to the worst abuses human beings are capable of, needs a parallel life that includes the best that people can be. That I have survived such a life and reached the age of 76, relatively sane if slightly grumpy, is due to having found in the past, thanks to my parents, teachers and professional colleagues, many of those humanising elements that provide balance – music, art, friendships, family and not least the calming influence of a canal boat.

Once I retired I deregistered as a professionally qualified social worker, which means I cannot practise in that role or give professional advice. This book is a memoir which traces the events of my life to the present including within my professional career. Therefore, I have been careful to describe my experiences, and where I am commenting on professional practice or on reports, or in relation to theoretical concepts that can be referenced, the memoir only reflects my personal view.

It has also been necessary to disguise or reduce the detail of the case material used in the book, in relation to court orders or where information has not appeared in the public domain, to preserve confidentiality. Where a report has been put in the public domain comment has to be restricted to coincide with those public statements.

Lastly, some readers may feel this book strays from memoir to polemic and back again, which may or may not be a fair criticism. However, if I am to reflect on my life and career then the values that underpin my experience need to be clear. Similarly, other readers may feel that I have included too much detail around child abuse. I would, however, ask readers to remember that what has been included is a tiny proportion of the reality; but none of us can hope to begin to understand the subject unless we face the pain that children who are abused have to face, day in day out.

Chapter 1 - A Moment in Time

Wretched as were the little companions and misery
he was leaving behind, they were the only friends he
had ever known and a sense of his loneliness in the
great wide world sank into the child's heart for the
first time.
Charles Dickens, Oliver Twist (1837)

I was aged nearly four when I was first confronted with child abuse. The year was 1946.

Some months earlier, my mother had become ill with TB. As was common at that time, her treatment consisted of surgery to remove sections of her lungs, followed by isolation in a sanatorium with plenty of bed rest and fresh air. In effect she was waiting to die because my father could not afford the drugs she needed.

During the early months of my mother's illness, my father coped with two young children with the help of friends and neighbours, whilst working as a maintenance and repair engineer in a factory in South London. He worked every minute of overtime that he could to earn enough to pay my mother's hospital bills, there being no National Health Service. After some months, when it became clear that more help was needed to cope with two young children, my father engaged a live-in housekeeper. From the outset she was a cold stern woman, which was bad enough, but after a few weeks she began a ritual that, although I did not know it at the time, would influence the rest of my life.

Every day, while my two-year-old brother, Peter,

was asleep in a room in another part of the rambling flat, the housekeeper would take me into a bedroom, undress me and tie me face down on a bed. She would let out the most blood-curdling screams and beat my bare body with a leather belt, dragging the brass buckle across my skin. The pain was indescribable and the first time I cried. This was a mistake and drove her into an increasing frenzy, screaming that if I cried she would hit me harder. I learnt not to cry. When she was finished the housekeeper would bathe me in very hot water which, because my skin was broken, would exacerbate the pain. Then I was put to bed with the same words ringing in my ears each time: "You must never tell anyone because if you do you will be taken away from your father and he will be sent to prison". Paralysed as it was with fear, my young mind failed to grasp the illogicality of that statement.

The months went by with no let-up in the beatings. If anything, they increased, until one day my father came home early from work and walked in on the housekeeper beating me. My father was a loving gentle man and it is hard to imagine what went through his mind when he walked into the house that day, but he did sack the housekeeper on the spot. I remember my father untied me, then gently bathed my wounds, saying very little but with tears rolling down his face. He stayed home from work for a few days afterwards to care for me; he told everyone he was unwell.

Eventually, he had to go back to work, but not before he had taken my brother and me to stay with his relatives in South Wales, where he had been born and raised. He explained that he wanted to make sure we were properly cared for until my mother was well enough to come home. To me alone he said: "You must never tell anyone what happened with the housekeeper and especially not Mum as it would worry her and could make her ill again." I was to forget it ever happened.

We were cared for by our relatives, though not together. During the first few months I used to lie awake at night wondering if Dad was in prison. One day I asked an aunt if he was. She looked very puzzled at my question and explained that Dad was working in London to earn the money to pay for my mum's hospital treatment. I never raised the subject again. Neither did I ever talk about the beating, although once in adolescence I tried to broach the subject with my father who simply responded by saying: "I do not know what you are talking about". For him, walking in on that scene all those years ago had been too painful, a matter of shame and it was better forgotten. I have no idea whether he ever discussed these events with my mother, but she was a very astute woman and I believe she would have suspected that something had happened even if she did not know the detail.

As I write this I am seventy-six years of age, but that experience aged nearly four is as vivid today in my memory as if it had happened yesterday; yet I, like many before me and many since, made sure it stayed a secret, but it was to have a significant impact on my professional and personal life as an adult.

Chapter 2 – Don't Mention the War

Let him who thinks war is a glorious golden thing...
let him but look at a little pile of sodden grey rags
that cover half a skull.
Preface, Testament of Youth, Vera Brittain

"Don't mention the war" is a line from *Fawlty Towers* uttered by John Cleese and remembered and endlessly repeated by everyone who saw it. But having been born during the Second World War, this account of my life would be incomplete if I did not mention it.

I was born in 1942 in South London and in 1943 our house suffered significant bomb damage and our family was evacuated to Oxted in Surrey, which back then seemed a long way away but today is part of the London commuter belt. We were housed in a converted stable block attached to a grand manor house. The owners were not too happy about this obviously working-class family descending on their rural idyll. My father continued to commute to London to work in a munitions factory repairing and maintaining the machinery.

In May 1944 my brother was born at home and so has a claim to fame of being born in a stable. I have some vague memories of living there but one thing I do not remember, but which my mother used to tell me about, was that it was in the stable yard I uttered my first swear word at the age of three.

By 1945 Hitler's boffins had developed a V1 and a V2 rocket system that were fired at Britain from the other side of the channel and the principle of their use was that when they ran out of fuel they fell to earth and blew up whatever or whoever was on the landing spot (a kind of primitive drone). Very cruel weapons because civilians on the ground could hear them coming but when the engine stopped they had no idea whether it would land on them. Thousands of civilians were killed in this way.

The rockets were known colloquially in Britain as "doodlebugs" and the story goes that I was standing in the stable yard when to my mother's embarrassment I called out - "another bloody one coming over"! According to my mother, this is what my father called out in anger when a doodlebug was overhead, so he got the blame for my widening vocabulary. Because my father travelled into London every day he saw the devastation these rockets caused as he picked his way through fallen debris and the bodies being removed. He was also familiar with feeling the fear they induced. He hated working in a munitions factory knowing that what was being made would cause the same devastation to innocent civilians in Germany. This was not a popular view in the UK, and his anger about war went very deep, hence the invective from a man I rarely ever heard swear.

In 1945 the war in Europe ended and we moved back to Sydenham in South London, to a basement flat that would today be called a "garden flat" by estate agents, but which my father described as having facilities that included hot and cold water, most of it running down the walls. It was so damp that, in the absence of the availability of wallpaper, my father would stick brown paper on the walls and colour them with distemper (an early version of emulsion paint) but it soon peeled off.

The only heating was a coal fire with a bunker next to the scullery which had a coal hole at road level for the coalman to pour deliveries down. There was no bathroom, just a tin bath in front of the fire on Fridays, an outside lavatory (the words loo or toilet not in common use by the British back then) without toilet rolls, just strips of newspaper which in our house were the Daily Mirror or News of the World. It was here that we remained until my mother contracted TB and my brother and I moved to relatives in South Wales, although my father continued to live in this dreadful place, which was owned by a BBC continuity announcer.

During our stay in South Wales my brother and I lived apart with different aunts and uncles, three of my father's sisters, Dolly, Eva, Irene and their husbands, and a brother, Cliff and his wife - moving from one to the other every few months. Aunt Irene also had a daughter Maureen. When I started school I soon moved to another relative in the neighbouring village. They were good, very small, primary schools, where the teachers all knew you and watched over your welfare. Our relatives were all very kind to us and, for children born in London, living in the country was a new experience. As I write this all sorts of odd memories return, among them the milk being delivered, not in bottles as it was in London but in a milk churn in the back of an Austin Seven car. You took a jug out to the "milkman" and he would fill it from the churn with a ladle.

Spring brought verges in country lanes covered first with primroses and later with bluebells which everyone picked and brought home for the table. We were close to the edge of the Bristol Channel and Aunt Dolly's husband Frank had a rowing boat in which he used to go fishing and he sometimes took us for a trip out to a lighthouse on a rocky outcrop. Looking back this seems extraordinary given that the stretch of water has one of the largest tidal rises and falls in Europe with exceptionally strong and dangerous currents. But my uncle, then in his fifties, had been fishing in this way since he was a boy and knew the currents. Also, my Uncle Frank had a lathe in his shed which he made all sorts of things on and one Christmas made me a beautifully painted, fully sailed yacht.

Another uncle was a former professional footballer (despite having only one eye) with Newport County in the days when that club could hold its own in the football league. Most of my uncles worked on the railways: Severn Tunnel Junction, one of the biggest railway repair works in the age of steam, was not far away. Severn Tunnel was, and still is, the means of trains travelling under the River Severn between London and South Wales and it leaked and had to have a pumping station at Sudbrook, removing the water 24 hours a day. Because of the incline, trains sometimes needed more than one steam engine to haul the carriages through and it was not unheard of for trains to get stuck, with long delays resulting for those following. The uncle with the boat worked in the pumping station so I got to go down the shaft for a look, which for a small boy was hugely exciting and may explain why, even today, I get nostalgic over steam trains.

This uncle (Frank) had his elderly mother living with him and my aunt and she was a character. She smoked like a chimney, drank two pints of stout a day for medicinal reasons and had a flutter every day on the horses, winning more than she lost.

Even the reuniting of our family had to be delayed, because a week before my mother was discharged from hospital I contracted scarlet fever, which in those days was treated by admitting the patient to an isolation hospital. I was there for six weeks, with my mother only able to see me through a window and vice versa.

By the age of six and a half, I was living back

with my parents, and attending a London primary school. The head teacher asked my parents to attend the school because of concerns about me as I never spoke in the classroom to my form teacher, a rather belligerent female teacher. My mum tried talking with me and, although I was terrified of the teacher, could not say so. The head decided to move me to another class with a male teacher and the problem went away.

Our return to London meant that since my birth I had lived in seven different places, been cared for by six sets of carers, attended four schools, had six weeks in an isolation hospital and been separated from my Mum for three years (almost half my life) and separated from my brother for two years. It added up to twenty significant changes during the whole of that period.

In 1949, when my mother was able to come home from hospital, we moved back to the same flat which had likely played a big part in her contracting TB. By this time, it was in an even worse state, although, ironically, an old bath and ancient geyser had been added. Our lovely GP, an Indian who had stayed in the UK after the war, was appalled at the flat's condition. He pestered councillors, our MP, anyone who would listen to try to get us rehoused. Unfortunately, the bomb damage was so great in London that, even five years after the end of the war, despite the Labour Government's house building drive which is recognised historically as a major political achievement, many people continued to live in terrible conditions. However, in 1950 our GP together with our MP, did finally persuade the local authority to issue an order condemning the flat as unfit for human habitation, but it would be another five years before we were rehoused.

When I was nine, my dad introduced me to politics, when he took me to a general election "hustings".

Labour had won in 1950 with a small majority and had to call another election in 1951. Before the advent of television, the only way to communicate with the electorate was using the radio, newspapers (as biased then as they are now) and knocking on doors, or "hustings", when all the candidates in a constituency gathered on a platform in a public hall face to face with local people. On this occasion in 1951, the candidates assembled, and the hall was packed. Each candidate had time to make a short speech followed by questions from the floor.

What you need to understand about my dad is that he was fiercely Welsh, ensuring he retained his Welsh roots and sense of 'Welshness', and a traditional socialist. His political hero was Aneurin Bevan, Secretary of State for Health in the post-war government who piloted the bill through Parliament that gave us the National Health Service in 1948. My Dad always credited the introduction of the NHS with saving my mother's life and he would have been right because he could never have afforded the treatment she needed. There were drugs available for those who could afford them to treat TB, but they were experimental. They were financially out of reach for my father but when the NHS arrived my mother was given the option to take part in a drug trial of an antibiotic, *Streptomycin*, thanks to our GP, which subsequently cured her of TB in what was left of her lungs.

Aneurin Bevan was, like my father, Welsh, and a great orator. On the other side my Dad disliked Winston Churchill but grudgingly gave Churchill credit for leading the nation in a way that prevented Hitler winning the war; but he always maintained that Churchill was responsible for the violence by the army against the striking Welsh miners in 1910/11 which, allegedly, had resulted in deaths of miners. In fact, historians now accept that, whilst Churchill as Home Secretary ordered the troops in to keep order, there was no violence from the troops per se but there was resentment in the South Wales coalfield that troops were used at all. Resentment has continued to smoulder, for example Clement Atlee, when leader of the Labour Party in 1940, warned that he might not be able to support Churchill's appointment as Prime Minister as head of a government of national unity because of his association with events in Tonypandy. He subsequently relented. In the 1950 election campaign, Churchill, at a husting in Cardiff, was forced to defend himself over his actions forty years before. James Callaghan in 1978 caused consternation in the House of Commons when Churchill's grandson, also called Winston Churchill, replying to a routine question on miners' pay, was warned not to pursue "the vendetta of your family against the miners of Tonypandy". That resentment is now part of the mining history of South Wales and still surfaces from time to time. My father never forgave Churchill.

At the "hustings", which seemed exciting even if I did not understand what was going on, my Dad was one of several people who would jump up and heckle the candidates. His method of heckling was to suddenly stand up and shout out "what about the groundnut scheme?" and then sit down. The candidates would look perplexed, none were able to give any sort of answer and I am not sure the audience understood either.

Eventually the chair asked my father to explain about the groundnut scheme, which he did. Basically, it was a crazy government adventure which all governments seem to need to indulge in from time to time and which costs a lot of money. The government of the day invested millions in cultivating groundnuts in Tanganyika (an African country now part of United Republic of Tanzania), a scheme that was intended both to create jobs and make a lot of money for the British taxpayer. Of course, it did neither. Not the first or last stupid political investment. Why this scheme so exercised my father I did not understand at the time.

In 2013 Professor Anthony King and Ivor Crewe published a book called *Blunders of Our Government (1)* based on extensive research analysis and government papers. One of the earliest examples of a blunder they describe was the groundnut (peanuts) scheme, which confirmed my Dad's explanation but with more detail. The scheme was designed to cope with a post-war shortage of vegetable oil by planting groundnuts on a lavish scale in Tanganyika, one of Britain's colonies. According to King and Crewe, ministers and their advisers chose to plant "their nuts" in thousands of acres that lacked both proper soil and adequate rainfall. By the time the scheme was abandoned in 1951 losses totalled £36 million (worth about £36 billion today) at a time when the country, ravaged by war, was broke. What upset my father was not just the economics, bad as they were, but the appalling exploitation of African workers by a supposedly socialist government.

I not only got an introduction to politics and subsequently race relations, I also saw a side of my father I had not seen before, he was normally so mild, but I was beginning to learn that he had deeply held views. Unlike my mother, who won a scholarship to a prestigious private school matriculating (today we would equate it with A-Levels) aged 18, my father was basically uneducated having left school at thirteen but somehow soaked up an extraordinary amount of information rather like a sponge.

Other "treats" were trips on a tram and trolley bus to London Airport in Croydon (yes Croydon, there was no Heathrow) to see the planes (no jets, they had yet to arrive), which all seemed terribly exciting but so far out of reach. Rather like the few occasions when my Dad took my brother and I to see Mum in hospital in Sandbanks in Dorset towards the end of her illness, which meant going through Southampton Docks on the train and we caught glimpses of the two great ocean liners of the time, the Queen Mary and Queen Elizabeth.

Before Christmas 1951 I asked my parents for a bike, but my Mum said they could not afford to buy one. However, Christmas morning at the bottom of the bed was a shiny bike. I learnt later that my Dad found two rusty bikes with some parts missing, in a scrap yard. He had combined them into one, got off all the rust and painted it bright blue. The only problem was that it was full size, and I was aged nine! Somehow, I managed to learn to ride it, mainly by falling off frequently and getting back on again.

I was ten when I was taken to hear my first male voice choir and I could feel the specialness of the music, the harmonies – the Welshness of the occasion. It was like going to my first Welsh Rugby International as an adult, when a whole stadium resounded to 60,000 people singing Welsh music. It is quite unique and defies description because it is a feeling, an experience. Today, sixty-six years later, I still tingle when I hear a Welsh male voice choir, for the same reasons as my father did – I love the music and it locates my Welsh identity.

I had been used to what was regarded as a very good primary school, with a caring and enlightened head teacher, Mr France, who had banned the use of the cane when most schools made liberal use of it. He knew every child by name and always had something positive to say about each one. Right up until he died in his nineties I received a Christmas card every year.

It was also a school with some interesting, albeit eccentric, teachers. For example, Mr Hughes who taught us maths had a deadly aim with a hard blackboard duster or piece of chalk hurled across the classroom to the back of the head if he thought you were not paying attention, it hurt! Occasionally he would get his cane out but then remember the head had banned its use and put it away, we got the message anyway. But despite this, he did care about his pupils and wanted them to have an enriching class room experience and it was not unusual for him to stop a maths lesson, get out his wind-up gramophone and play us LPs of music composed by Mozart, which I thought was amazing. Other days he would suddenly, mid-way through a lesson, get us all singing a classical choral piece.

Although it would be many years before I took a real interest in music, this was where the seeds were sown. Mr Hughes was building on foundations created by my mother being a piano teacher and my father's love of male voice choirs, and he encouraged me to sing in the school choir, one of the highlights of our year was to sing in a massed schools choir concert in the Royal Albert Hall, which was broadcast on the Home Service on the "wireless" (radio).

There was also a teacher whose name was Epstein, who was Greek and had come to the UK during the war and taught history. He covered all the usual stuff, dates, kings and queens, but I think he used to get bored with this (we certainly did!) and he would launch into Greek mythology with all its exciting stories or produce drawings or pictures of ancient Greek architecture. All I know is that I was fascinated by these wonderful drawings of beautiful buildings such as the Parthenon and Temple of Zeus. Even though I had never been further than South Wales, I hoped one day I would see them. I finally got my wish in my early forties when I went to Athens to give the key note speech at a conference. The buildings were even more beautiful than the illustrations I'd been shown thirty years earlier.

Then there was a male teacher no one liked who, though equally unspoken, was my second, though not first hand, encounter with abuse. Every lesson he would invite one of the girls to go and sit on his lap for the first half of the lesson and another one for the second half and as he spoke he would put his hand up their skirt. We all knew something was wrong in the classroom, we described him as creepy, but we did not have the vocabulary or the concept of sexual abuse to understand or explain what was happening. No one would have believed us and so instead we became disruptive as a class which meant he had to stand up, so the girl would go back to her seat. Then he would send for the head who would tell us off and the cycle would begin again. Little has changed; even today people fail to believe children when they report abuse against professionals.

But there were a lot of very good teachers at the school and I was lucky to be in a primary school with a very good sports teacher who encouraged me to get involved in football and cricket, which for many years became a bit of an obsession and was to stand me in good stead when I went to secondary school.

In 1952, along with ninety percent of children, I failed my 11 plus examination so was not among the small number of state pupils to go to a grammar school, which was the only possible route to university later. So, at eleven years of age, I headed off to Heseltine Secondary Modern, a school with a fearsome reputation, known locally as the Gas Works Academy thanks to its location next to the gas works. Violence was the pervading culture, teenage gangs roamed the corridors and playgrounds, some carrying weapons like flick knives, and staff were powerless to deal with them. Pupils learnt quickly never to be alone anywhere because they would be set upon and there was relative safety in numbers. Education in terms of learning was for the most part non-existent. One bright spot was the art class where, despite the general atmosphere, an enthusiastic and positive teacher somehow instilled a love of the visual arts in the brains of some of us. And sport helped keep me away from trouble.

By now I had also started learning to cook, partly because when my mother's mobility was at its most impaired I had to help, and my father did most of the cooking. When my mum started cooking again, I helped her too.

Having been given a camera when I was 11, I had, unknowingly, already got the beginnings of a range of interests that would create essential balance in my life, offering calm contrasts to the effects of the heart-breaking abuse and neglect I encountered daily through my work.

On my last day at Heseltine the inspirational art teacher was stabbed by a 15-year-old pupil – politicians and the media talk a lot about violence in schools today, but it's not new and as a society we have failed to find any ways to curb these crimes.

Having left Heseltine, I was due to go to a technical school, but it had to be delayed for six months when I was diagnosed during the school summer holiday with a dislocated right hip. I had not had an accident, but the bones had not grown correctly, which was put down to the fact that I weighed eleven stone at thirteen despite playing a lot of sport. Within a week I had an operation, experimental on a child at the time, to insert a six-inch pin into the hip and thigh bone. The surgeon told my parents that it would have to come out when I was fully grown and that I would probably have arthritis later in life. He was wrong about the pin, which is still in place, but the arthritic prediction was correct.

For six months I used crutches and the local authority provided me with a teacher at home three mornings a week for maths and English. In the middle of this period we were finally rehoused. Lewisham Borough Council had built some new flats on Horniman's Hill next to Horniman's Museum in Forest Hill. There were four blocks of six flats and we had a ground floor two-bedroom flat. After what we were used to, these brand-new facilities seemed like luxury. The downside for my father was that he would no longer have a garden and he not only loved gardening, but he grew all our vegetables. There was, however, a balcony and over the years he lived there he filled it with pots growing only sweet peas. So tall did they grow the people upstairs could cut flowers as well. But my father felt the loss of the garden was worth it for my mother finally to have a comfortable place to live all on one level. There is no doubt that having moved, my mother's health and wellbeing improved greatly, though she never fully regained her health and mobility.

Before her illness my mother had been a piano teacher and on moving into the new flat, my father somehow purloined a piano for her to play again, her original one having been lost when our house was bombed. My mother started playing again and in the evenings my father would ask her to play and the flat was filled with music. My mum tried to teach me to play but by then I was into cricket and football and not keen on the practice. I know she was disappointed and now when I hear my daughter, Mairion, a very good pianist, playing, the fact I did not learn is one of my few regrets.

Living in Forest Hill was very different for all sorts of reasons, the trams passing by outside on their way into central London, the museum next door, bands that played on the bandstand in the local park, my mother becoming stronger and starting to become more mobile and my friends from primary school, Colin Straker and Brian Somers among them, were still very much a part of my life and helped a great deal while I was on crutches.

It was also around this time that my dad got caught up in a dispute at work. Anyone who can remember the early fifties will remember the controversy surrounding the immigration into the UK of people from the Caribbean. The arrival of the first ship, the MV Empire Windrush in 1948 was followed by others with a total of 40,000 new immigrants by 1956. The new incoming residents from the Caribbean were part of a scheme to bring in additional workers to fill the vacancies left by those killed during the war. A new Act of Parliament was passed in 1948 (2) and fully implemented in 1951 by the new Conservative Government.

The factory my dad worked in had agreed to take a number of Jamaican workers, but the union objected and instructed their members to have nothing to do with the immigrant workers, telling them that they should be "sent to Coventry", not a phrase you often hear these days, but which meant essentially that no union member should talk to or socialise with the new workers.

My dad was appalled, as was my mum, and he

refused to comply with the union instruction, so he was "sent to Coventry" as well. Today people argue over an immigration influx of Poles, Romanians or Bulgarians, forgetting about the thousands of ex-pats who have moved to France, Spain or Italy and live in their national groups, never integrating but expecting all the benefits and services on offer to be made available as of right.

Rather than falling into line, my dad befriended this group of newcomers and suddenly I was meeting black faces in our home, something I had never seen before. They were great fun and they played cricket, one of my passions by this time, and one of them actually knew members of the West Indian cricket team, how brilliant was that?

My father stuck to his guns for several months and eventually the dispute just fizzled out and things returned to normal, but the Jamaican workers never forgot my dad's support. They introduced him to rum and whenever one of them went home for a holiday there was a large bottle of genuine Jamaican rum for my dad on their return. More significantly for me, I saw my parents standing up against racism even when my father was ostracised by his white colleagues and refusing to give in when he believed a group of people was being treated badly. All this had quite an impact on me and was another significant influence on my attitudes and is a theme I will return to in Chapter Nine.

During this time politics was regularly discussed at home. From time to time the subject of the Holocaust came up and I vividly remember my mother and father sometimes crying when they talked about it because of the losses incurred by their Jewish friends, another theme I shall return to in Chapter Nine.

Once off crutches I moved to my new school, but there had been change. The South-East London

Secondary Technical School was a very successful institution with a direct link into the South-East London Technical College and I was looking forward to starting. My father was so pleased, seeing this as a means to a secure future, but neither my parents nor I were familiar with the way education authorities sometimes have a rush of blood to the head and make crass decisions based on foolish organisational theory and cost cutting...

At some point prior to me taking the entrance exam, the Inner London Education authority decided to amalgamate my new successful school with two failing secondary modern schools, on three sites, under one management team. Sound familiar? The school I thought I was going to, which had a good reputation, was being amalgamated with two of what today would be described by politicians and media as "sink schools", with the management team in one of the latter schools. The stated aim was for the good school to pull up the quality in the other two schools. No one will be surprised to learn that in practice it worked the other way around, with the good school being pulled down to the level of the other two.

The culture in the school was very like the one I had just left, with disaffected teachers and some who bullied students. Because of the surgery I'd had, I was late starting, and the surgeon had been very clear with my parents that I was not to do sport or games for at least twelve months after coming off crutches. Yet when I went to my new school the PE teacher, a former Sergeant Major in the army, would not accept that the surgeon's letter sent to the school explaining why I should not do any PE had any relevance and he forced me to join in. When I went home and told my mum, who was a very placid woman and not given to being outspoken, it was clear from the look on her face that she was not pleased.

Sitting in a class the following day I noticed my mum walking slowly across the playground, which was a complete shock. Bearing in mind her impaired mobility, she had made the five-mile journey on three different buses followed by a quarter of a mile walk at the end to get there. Somehow, I knew this was no ordinary school visit and a few minutes later I was summoned to the head teacher's office where I was told that I was not under any circumstances to do any sport or PE and if the teacher tried to insist I was to go and tell the head.

I have no idea what my mum said to the head, but given she was sitting there struggling for breath (and he knew about her health and where we lived) I can only assume her anger must have been very clear. I was then given the rest of the day off to take her home and a teacher arranged transport to the bus stop. My mum had not told my father what she was going to do, and he was amazed when she told him, and he gave her a big hug, not something they were prone to do in front of me.

School had always been a trial, especially learning to read. I found that words seemed jumbled up and appeared to move around as though they were shimmering. The result was that if I was asked to read out loud in class I stumbled over the words and, if I tried to read on my own, it was alright for a few minutes but then all the shimmering began. Somehow, I learnt to screw up my eyes, which improved what I could see, but reading was still difficult. Reading is the cornerstone of education and I therefore struggled through most subjects, the big exception being art.

However, at fourteen, I had been part of a group of boys that played football together and we decided to form our own club and join a local junior league. I found myself looking after the paper work the league required, to meet the requirements of the Football

Association. The club did very well and continued long after I moved on.

Similarly, the same group formed a cricket team with help from a local school teacher, but we ran into an initial and unexpected controversy, a girl wanted to join. The reader needs to remember this was the 1950s and the idea a girl would play cricket was unheard of. The girl, Jean, used to practise in the nets with myself and another boy, and she was brilliant. She could bat most of the boys off the park and was a superb fielder. The team was not impressed with the idea, but the two of us who had practised with her kept on at the rest until they gave in and it became clear very quickly she was going to be our best batter. To see Jean "belt a ball to the boundary" and winding up the opposition in the process was something to behold. Unfortunately, she discovered boys and gave up cricket.

My time at secondary school was short lived. I left, along with all the pupils in my year, at the age of 15. In terms of education it was a time when I learnt little. None of those leaving sat any O-Levels (the precursor to GCSEs), as we were not considered intelligent enough to do so. On my final day in school my form tutor said goodbye with the words: *"It's just as well you are leaving Fitzgerald, because the only thing you are fit for is sticking labels on jam pots"*. So, with those words ringing in my ears I set forth to earn my fortune. I did not earn a fortune, but I am sorry that my form tutor had died before I had my first book published because it would have given me great satisfaction to send him a signed copy with a suitably cryptic comment.

Chapter 3 – Out into the World of Work

"What is really important in education is not that the child learns this and that, but that the mind is matured, that energy is aroused."
Søren Kierkegaard

Fortunately, before I left school, the Inner London Careers Service had picked me up (there was such a service in those days) and I was interviewed by one of their officers who asked me, amongst other things, what sort of company I would like to join. My answer was one with a good cricket and football club. It's hard to imagine saying that in an interview today but in the late fifties work was plentiful and most big companies had sports clubs and wanted to employ people who were good at sport to represent the company, so my answer to the question was not as "off the wall" as it might seem now.

The careers officer set up an appointment with a company called Kearley & Tonge, which was looking to recruit new tea boys and girls. At the time they were the largest food wholesalers in the country as well as owning a large chain of food shops, a tea-producing company called Ridgways, a jam factory in Brentford and an import and export business. Their headquarters were in Mitre Square on the Eastern edge of the city of London, an area that was frequented by Jack the Ripper with some of his murders committed there (I hasten to add long before I was born). At my interview I was asked why I wanted to join the company. I told them it was because they had a good cricket and football club, and they promptly offered me a job. I left school on the Friday and started work as a tea boy on the Monday. Part of the terms and conditions of employment was that out of my first month's wages (my pay was £2.50 a week) I had to buy a suit and out of my second month's salary a second one!

There were 12 tea boys and girls whose job it was to keep the huge office block supplied with liquid refreshment throughout the day, but not before we had been sent on a training course on how to make tea. As a producer of fine teas, the company was very particular about the quality of the tea its staff drank and there were a number of things to learn. We were given lectures on the growing of different types of tea, we were asked to take part in a tasting of various teas, but the two most important things drummed into us were a) warm the pot and b) do not boil the kettle but remove from the heat just before it reaches boiling point; we were told that boiling water kills the flavour. The trainers then made us taste tea made at boiling point and that made just before, and they were right!

Around this time my interest in the visual arts gathered pace. As I have already mentioned, my interest began with a very good art teacher in secondary school but got really fired up in an unlikely place. I was around sixteen, a member of a youth club, and one of the leaders was the PA to the then Director of the Tate. He came to the club to talk about painting and painters; a less likely audience for the subject than this pimply group of adolescents would be hard to find. But something happened. He was an animated and enthusiastic speaker who really knew how to use photographs and to enthuse. His description of the likes of Monet, Picasso, Van Gogh, and Rembrandt was captivating. I was hooked but again it would be another twenty years before I would develop any of these interests.

I stayed with the company for three and half years and it was while working for them that my interest in steel narrow boats began. Having graduated from being a tea boy to an errand boy, my boss would send me off on errands all over London, taking things to, or collecting things from, shops, factories and warehouses. Occasionally I would be sent to the company's jam factory in Brentford, thankfully not to stick labels on jam pots, and the factory was on the side of the Grand Union Canal. I was fascinated to see up to ten working narrow boats moored unloading sugar or loading jam pots, something which happened every day.

Throughout my time with Kearley and Tonge I had a senior member of staff who looked after me, a Mr Whittear, who made sure I was content and was always available to answer questions. As time went by he also introduced me to new types of work, today we would probably call it mentoring. After a few months I was moved to the buying office which had high Dickensian desks, stools and ink wells, though no quill pens! My mentor, was, I think, astute – he realised I had problems with words and numbers, but he clearly felt there were things I was good at.

The company's policy was to expose young staff to as much different work as possible so that they could progress through the company and form a long-term career. During that period, I learnt about all sorts of things I would never otherwise have come across, stem ginger and lychees just two of them. I had never heard of either until I was given the job of setting regular tastings for buyers. Christmas crackers occupied me at the beginning of January because it was then I had to lay out the display for buyers to come in and choose which ones they wanted for their stores the following Christmas. Blue is my favourite colour and I remember being disappointed every year when buyers rarely chose blue crackers, the colour was considered too cold.

However, sport was important to the company because they hoped that from amongst their many activities and teams, successful sports men and women would emerge who could act as ambassadors for the company. At that stage I was quite good at cricket, so I found myself moving from the lower ranking teams to the first team very quickly, which meant I would be playing for the company four times a week, twice at weekends and twice during the week, meaning that in effect I only worked a three-day week during the summer.

But cricket got me into trouble on two fronts. The first time when I was a teenager and a member of the Boys' Brigade which met for bible class on a Sunday, but I had to play cricket for the company on that day. I was given an ultimatum by the Boys' Brigade, give up cricket or leave. I left!

Then, when I was eighteen I got into trouble over cricket with the company when Essex County Cricket Club offered me terms on a new professional scheme for young players, the game having been amateur until then. The offer came through the company and would have meant I was released from my job during the summer but kept on the payroll so as to return to work in the winter. I shocked the company by turning Essex down. I loved playing cricket and may have been good enough to become an average county player but not good enough to go beyond that and I felt that playing in mostly empty grounds with no possibility of developing beyond that would be soul destroying.

I was cricket mad and I did have a dream of being the next Fred Trueman and playing for England, but at 5ft 8ins tall I would never have the height to create the speed and bounce as a bowler to succeed at that level and my batting skills were never going to be good enough. The company was shocked, so much so I was summoned to the Managing Director's office, given a lecture on loyalty to the company and asked to reconsider, with it being made clear if I did not accept I could not expect to progress any further with the organisation.

I talked the problem over with my parents who were torn because they could see that while I would not be happy accepting the Essex offer I would be throwing away a guaranteed career if I didn't. My father found this extremely hard because he and his extended family had lived through the great depression of the 1930s and had long periods out of work, but both he and my mother said they would support me whatever decision I made. I turned the offer down. Do I regret it? Not really. As time went by I played a lot of cricket at a level which I could enjoy. My biggest disappointment was knowing that I would now need to find another job because I had enjoyed working for the company. Ironically, my younger brother, Peter, was a much more talented cricketer and footballer who, had he continued, would easily have become a successful sports person.

Despite my obsession with cricket I also became part of a skiffle group. For younger readers, skiffle was a cross between rock and roll and Country and Western music. I tried learning to play a guitar but was not very good and was promoted to play the washboard (used pre-washing machines), with metal thimbles on each finger to both protect my digits and make a louder noise. When something more exotic was required I was a virtuoso on the comb and paper.

In 1961 I moved to Shell Mex and BP in Newport (Monmouthshire) as a routing clerk, which meant working out the routes for petrol, diesel and fuel oil tankers to deliver supplies to garages and factories across South Wales and as far north as Hay-on-Wye. There were no motorways, few dual carriageways, and lots of low bridges, narrow forecourts and small companies located down narrow tracks. This meant using a fleet of vehicles of varying sizes to full advantage. We were based in Newport docks, which really played into my pleasure at being near water and boats, another of the constant themes in my life.

I also worked with some nice people and some eccentric garage owners. One used to ring up when he had run out because he never checked his stock and expected us to somehow bail him out, which we usually did. The first time I spoke to him, knowing I had moved from London, he asked 'have you seen the lights of *Llwynypia*,' in the mining community of South Wales, which he claimed were far better than those in Blackpool. I thought he was being serious until I enquired of my colleagues who fell about laughing. Next time he called he suggested I should visit the treacle mines at Pontypridd!

After that I moved to the wages office in a haulage company. Let's just say I was a particularly inept wages clerk. I could never get the calculations right and caused chaos and it was clearly not for me. During my five years in South Wales I had become involved in running a youth club and as my career in a wages office looked like ending in humiliation, I began to think it might be better to consider "working with people" although I had no idea how to achieve this. In 1966 I married for the first time and as work in South Wales was in short supply thought there might be more opportunities back in London.

Then I saw an advert with the Children's Society, applied and got the job. From a career perspective this was to be a turning point. When I went for interview the first person I met was the personnel officer's PA, Maureen Fitzgerald, same name so that was encouraging. I was given a Dictaphone on my first morning and this changed the world of work for me because spelling, reading, words and grammar had always been problematic and now someone else was looking after that for me. However, I did have to learn to check letters and reports carefully when they came back from the typist: I once dictated in a letter that the issue should be referred to the local vicar and his wife and it came back from the typist as the pathetic vicar and his wife, but maybe she knew him!

In the early sixties the Children's Society had a large headquarters building in Kennington near the Oval, which was good news for a cricket nut. Most of the staff were women with only a tiny number of men, making it a very different working environment to those I had been used to. I must say most were welcoming and only one or two were clearly unhappy at my presence initially.

Over the next five years I was given opportunities to do a range of interesting work administering the society's activities with children in residential care, foster care and adoption and it eventually convinced me that what I really wanted to do was to train as a social worker, and so began the process that led me into further education and a professional career that was to take me on a rollercoaster ride into areas of life I had previously known little about, but it was not easy.

I started applying to professional social work courses towards the end of 1968 at a time when professional qualifications were new, and some courses were designed for what were defined as mature students. With my lack of qualifications, I didn't get to the starting gate with major universities and had to look at colleges of further education. I didn't make much progress there either until a course in Maidstone at the end of the application process turned me down but put me on their reserve list in case anyone who had been offered a place dropped out, but they added that this was rare.

I was feeling a bit downhearted by this time and went to talk to the deputy director of the Children's Society, Winifred Stone, who suggested I should not give up yet. After all, she said, the Society had faith in me and was going to pay me a salary through college. I should start the application rounds again, she said. That cheered me up, but I did not have any qualifications and knew that was not helping me. But before I could do anything about new applications I got a letter in mid-August 1969 from the Maidstone course saying someone *had* dropped out and would I like their place, starting in a month's time.

I went to see Winifred Stone who was delighted for me, even though it meant she had little time to find a replacement for me. My mum and dad were so proud that at last someone in the family had made it into college, albeit a College of Technology, even if they had had to wait until I was twenty-eight.

Reflecting on that development now three things strike me. Firstly, if I was twenty-eight today, without any qualifications, I would not be accepted for professional social work training. Secondly, if I had enough qualifications, whilst some employers would make payments, I would be saddled with a debt upwards of £50,000 plus iniquitous interest rates of six per cent when bank rate is around one per cent to pay for university fees. Thirdly, how badly, therefore, we treat the current generation of students. At least in Wales, but not in England, students are eligible for means tested maintenance grants, but it's not enough if you come from a low-income background. It is my generation which had a far better deal, that has let down our current young people.

Shortly afterwards the formal offer arrived, together with an extensive reading list and the enormity of what I was trying to do hit me. My secondary school career had been a non-event. I'd learned little, and I had not undertaken any formal study since. How was I going to learn how to study? Many years later my first marriage ended in a painful divorce, but it would be wrong not to acknowledge here that my first wife Molly, who had gone to grammar school and got a full set of A-levels, and a very special tutor on the first year of the course, Pearl Jones, showed me not only how to learn but to understand the process that makes it possible. Whatever my shortcomings with the written word at that stage, they showed me the way to overcome the problem and I am therefore in debt to both of them.

For me the two-year course was a fabulous time, opening up a way of looking at the world that was exciting and humbling. Exciting because of the process of learning and humbling because social work was, and is, about people's lives and the pain they go through. In many ways it was an experimental course as such courses were relatively new. The breadth of subjects was overwhelming, at first, but in time became both stimulating and eye opening, ranging from Psychoanalysis, to Child Psychiatry, Law, Paediatrics, Sociology to Social Administration which was more like social history and politics.

It was also a time of meeting new people. It was a small intake, just sixteen, but we were all classified as mature students though I sometimes wondered how accurate that was! Two people I met on the course have remained both friends and colleagues, Joyce Brand and Wendy Alsop. We share similar values in relation to working with children and families, to the organisation of Children's Services, to the need for far more therapeutic services than are available especially for children. So much so, that even now, 47 years after qualifying, we can pick up immediately where we left off with the result that both have played a significant part in my life and whose company I enjoy immensely.

It wasn't all hard work in college. There was a lot of sport available with facilities meaning that tennis and badminton featured largely in the extra-curricular activities and, playing most days as I did, I don't think I have been so physically fit before or since.

One of the things I felt I was extremely lucky about was the quality of placements I was given. In my first term we were all sent to primary schools for two days a week for one term to observe children in their everyday life. I was not sure beforehand what I could get out of it, but I was allocated to a brilliant infants' teacher who was as curious about the process as I was. Afterwards I was absolutely sure that the placement was a perceptive way of focusing my mind on real children and not theoretical models.

Another placement in a Probation Department (when the probation service meant something) taught me so much, not least how fallible I was. I was allocated a case in which a teenage boy had committed a series of petty offences and his father had thrown him out. When I interviewed both they were equally adamant they did not want anything to do with each other. My report to the court, which in those days you had to read out, concluded that there was no hope of reconciliation and the boy would need long term care with help to address his offences.

When I sat down the father stood up and asked to say something. He said he wished to apologise to the court and to me for not coming forward earlier but after my visit to his home he had gone to see his son in residential care and they had decided both had been wrong. They were now reconciled, and the boy had been back at home for two weeks and he again apologised for not telling me. The magistrate, with a twinkle in his eye, asked: "Do you have anything to say in the light of these circumstances Mr Fitzgerald before sentencing?" I staggered to my feet and muttered something about being pleased at this turn of events and suggested a supervision order and sat down. The magistrate said, "I think that would be best and we hope all of your visits to defendants' homes will have such dramatic results in future!"

My final placement was in a former children's department in Gravesend with a great bunch of staff. My supervisor used the placement to "stretch me"; giving me one case that had been hanging around for a long time. A health visitor was expressing concerns about neglect by a single mother of just one of her three children which would in itself be unusual. When I went to the home and I saw the child that health visitors were worried about; I could see why. It was mid-afternoon and the child, who was eighteen months old, was half asleep on the settee looking rather pale with the mother sitting at the other end of the settee while two other children under five raced around the room.

The mother told me she had asked the health visitor to arrange for the doctor to come because her little boy was too poorly to take to the surgery which was two miles away and she did not have any transport. I agreed to talk to both the health visitor and GP and get back to her.

When I talked to the health visitor she said she had tried to get the GP to visit but he had refused on the grounds that all the families on that estate neglected their children and it would be a waste of time going to see them. I then talked to the GP who made similar comments, saying I should talk to the health visitor and then put the phone down. The following morning, after talking it through with my supervisor, I went back to see the family. The child was on the settee and even sleepier and looking worse than the day before with the mother looking even more exhausted. I explained that I was going to a phone box (no mobile phones then) to make a call and then I'd be back. I called my supervisor and explained that the child had deteriorated overnight; I told him that I did not think we could wait for a negotiation with the GP but that I should put the whole family in my car and take them to hospital and I asked if he could call the hospital to let them know we were on our way.

We got to the hospital and were whisked in to see a consultant paediatrician who was alarmed that the child was seriously ill and started to ask why the mother had not brought the boy in before now. I interrupted and explained there had been several attempts by both the mother and a health visitor to get a GP to visit, but he had refused to do so. The paediatrician arranged an immediate admission and tests. Meanwhile, my supervisor had arrived to tell me an angry GP was on his way as he considered I had no right to take the children to hospital. At this the paediatrician said that he would deal with the GP. We overheard the dressing down the GP was given and it was made very clear I had acted correctly given that he had refused to visit when I asked him to.

When the test results came back a few days later they showed the child had an incurable cancer with little time left. The tests also confirmed that had he been seen earlier no treatment could have been provided, but he could certainly have been made comfortable and help provided to care for him and his siblings, which is what was then done. He died three weeks later.

The experience was harrowing for me, but nothing

like as harrowing as it was for the mother and child, and in talking it over with my supervisor he helped me see there was nothing more I could have done. He said that I should remember that I had made a difference. He also commented that we have to work with other professionals but sometimes they are wrong, and we need to act in the best interests of the child even if it makes us unpopular.

These were the days when social workers had a lunch break, and, in the placement, it was often spent playing tennis or badminton. One of the people I played with was a young social worker from Scotland called Hilary who was better than me. Hilary subsequently became a teacher and successful head teacher back in Scotland. I cannot help feeling that having a proper break midday is far better for our wellbeing as opposed to eating a sandwich at the desk or in the car and for most of my working life I stuck to a real lunch break.

There was a glitch at the college when too many of the best tutors left very suddenly to be replaced by a motley bunch but, fortunately for me, Mary Gordon remained and because we were out on placement three days a week, the impact of these changes was minimal.

The course was stressful. The last serious exam I had taken was my 11+ and no amount of assurance could convince me I could cope with exams, the writing of essays I found excruciating in the first year. But I was getting good marks with a good collection of "As" and there were the seminar presentations that had to be made. By the time we got to the end I was convinced I was going to fail. Even my final year tutor Mary Gordon (who had been brilliant with me and my eccentric approach all the way through) telling me I had worked so hard and had a lot "of credit in the bank" that even a slip up in my final exam should not affect the final result, but this did not convince me. But she was right, I did not slip up.

When my training came to an end I felt I had learnt a great deal of theory, but the practice placements exposed how much there was still to learn and how much there is that we will never fully understand.

Chapter 4 - A New Career

How much I have suffered is, as I have said already,
utterly beyond my power to tell but I kept my own
counsel and did my work.
Charles Dickens, My Early Times (Folio Society 1988)

The training was over, a short holiday and then it was
back to a new job with the Children's Society as one
of a small number of professionally qualified social
workers based in a team that covered the whole of
South London and down to the coasts of Sussex and
Kent. Initially I was working on cases of children
in residential care and with families to keep their
children out of the system. Although the organisation
was the biggest adoption agency in the UK, I was not
allowed into the adoption arena because I was a man.
Traditionally, adoption placements were dealt with
by women and there was a heated debate going on
inside the Children's Society about whether this new-
fangled qualified social worker and a man to boot
should be allowed in.

Subsequently, it was agreed that I could do so
for a probationary six-month period as long as I was
supervised by an experienced female social worker. As
it happened, my supervisor, Mary Randall, fulfilled all
those criteria as well as being professionally qualified.
Mary thought the whole debate was farcical, which it
was, but we both knew the old system found change
difficult to cope with and therefore this was a way of
breaking the log jam. By the time the six months were
up everyone had forgotten the debate.

Adoption work within the Society in 1971 was about the placement of babies with infertile couples and the process of matching babies and families was rather simplistic. An administrator matched up social background, colour of hair, eyes, skin and parental features and that was about it. I was not really happy with this, especially as it was all done by post, and I said that before details of babies were passed to couples I was dealing with I wanted to go and see the baby in the residential nursery, talk to the staff and if possible the birth parent(s) so that I could have a half way intelligent conversation with the potential parents. It was an idea that went down like a "lead balloon".

The first time I went off to a nursery to see a baby it just so happened that a very formidable matron ruled the roost. As I arrived at the nursery the matron opened the door, greeting me very gruffly. I was shown into a room with about twenty cots (ghastly) and the matron said to a nursery nurse, "This is Mr Fitzgerald. He has come to see baby X and under no circumstances must he be allowed to touch the baby." The very young nursery nurse looked terrified. Then the matron went to the door of the room, looked down the corridor and yelled at another young nursery nurse who came scurrying along. The matron introduced me and told the nursery nurse that under no circumstances was I to be left alone with Nurse Y. She then left the room and the two nurses relaxed.

Of course, the matron was right to be aware of potential problems as most abusers are men, but there are ways of doing things. After that incident, being a strange creature, a man, in a predominantly women's world, seemed to worry the female professional and administrative staff less and I had no problems with nurseries or anyone else after that. But, over the years, I have reflected on this and the fact that, whatever anxieties and prejudices women in the organisation had about the appointment of a man to undertake adoption work, they disappeared very quickly. Suppose the boot had been on the other foot and the organisation employed predominantly men and a woman came along to do what was perceived as a male occupation, would they have been as generous? The answer is an emphatic "no".

Down the years, despite the efforts of feminism, women still do not have equality in the work place, or most of our institutions. Never a week goes by when women don't have to resort to employment tribunals to receive justice. All of our political institutions are dominated by men with the percentage of women MPs still very small and too many male MPs behave like boorish misogynists. Or what of the Church of England and the ridiculous objections, first to women priests and subsequently bishops.

For many years I was employed in female-dominated work places but have been treated for the most part with a generosity of spirit, it really is time the male of the species recognised it is behaving badly, rectify that behaviour and stop defending the indefensible.

One of the families I inherited on my case load was a single woman, originally from Sri Lanka, with three children, the youngest of whom had been badly scalded, it was thought by her mother. As a result, all three children were removed. The dilemma was that everyone who knew the family was suspicious about the circumstances in which the child had been burnt, but none of them could "put their finger" on why, as the mother would not discuss it. I made six visits to the home and got nowhere, conversation was non-existent and answers to questions monosyllabic or answered with a shake of the head. I sensed there was more to what had happened but had no information to back up my instincts.

At a case conference I said that, although I sensed there was more, I could add nothing to what was already known except that I wondered if her reaction to social workers was the result of fear. It was decided the children would not go home and a long term permanent family would be sought for them and I was given the task of going to discuss it with the mother. My line manager asked me if I could take along a young American student who was on placement with us.

When we arrived at the home my breezy American student immediately started talking to the mother about Sri Lanka, which she had visited, and the young woman started to relax. I was despatched to make the tea and by the time I was handing it out my student said, *"There's something that X wants to say to you."* To cut a very long story short, it transpired that it was not the mother who was responsible for the child's injuries but her landlord. He had been pestering her and turned up when she had just boiled some water, demanded sex, and when she refused he picked up the saucepan and poured the boiling water over the child and threatened that if she told anyone he would come back and do the same to her. Subsequently the landlord was arrested and convicted, and the mother was reunited with her children.

Although we had all sensed something was wrong, we had not been able to find a way to communicate and it really was only luck that the student had been to Sri Lanka. Strictly speaking she should not have initiated the conversation, merely followed my lead. But if she had behaved how she should have done, would we have got to the heart of the problem? Probably not. However, with the benefit of hindsight, I question whether assigning a male social worker to the case, me, was sensible. We know that women who have been threatened, abused or coerced by men live in fear of us but the previous social worker had been a woman. It was the breezy approach of the student who had been to Sri Lanka that had "unlocked the door". It made me think long and hard about the need to be alive to the possibility that the people I was dealing with might have suffered abuse, all kinds of assaults and to make sure identity and culture were considered.

One part of South London in which I worked had a sizable population of people who had moved here from Nigeria, amongst whom were ten single mothers whose children were in residential children's homes. I was given the task of trying to work out whether or not we would be able to find a way to return their children to them. Reading through the families' files, I found their experiences had a lot of similarities, but four things stood out.

All ten women had Nigerian husbands who had come to this country alone to study, leaving their spouses behind. Once settled, the men sent for their wives and very quickly they became pregnant. Eventually, once the men's studies were coming to an end, the mothers were admitted to the same psychiatric hospital and the children were placed in residential care. In each case, following their wives' admission to a psychiatric hospital, the fathers returned permanently to Nigeria. As a narrative it was very worrying but worse still was the psychiatric diagnosis given to these unfortunate women: schizophrenia.

Today, we know that people from ethnic minority backgrounds are over represented in psychiatric hospitals and prisons, but this was 1972 when such thinking was not on any agenda. However, looking at these stories alarmed me; could a group of ten women all from Nigeria living in one community all be suffering from schizophrenia? It did not seem credible. I discussed it with my senior and then Winifred Stone and agreed that as a narrative it "did not stand up". We set up a meeting with the hospital, including the mothers' psychiatrist. It was a very difficult discussion and we seemed to make little progress, with it being made very clear that the psychiatric staff knew best as they were the professionals with responsibility for these women. Winifred Stone, my senior and I went home very depressed by the outcome.

The following morning, I got a call from the psychiatrist who had been at the meeting, a young woman about the same age as me, asking for another meeting that day. When we met she told me that she had had a sleepless night thinking about what we had said and gone to the hospital to check her files and she had reluctantly come around to our view that such a group all suffering from schizophrenia was not credible. To cut a very long story short, the psychiatrist and hospital staff reassessed the mothers and concluded that what staff had logged as schizophrenia was wrong and that our perspective that they had been brought to the UK, an alien environment, had been kept isolated and then abandoned, unable to cope leading to deep unhappiness and, in some cases, clinical depression, was the correct one.

Over the next few months with help from Social Services, the Housing Department, the hospital and our team we were able to return these women into the community with a support network and eventually their children went home to live with them. They all remained in the UK. This situation had a lasting impact on me, my immediate colleagues and hospital staff.

After about nine months I was given the role of social worker to St Luke's children's therapeutic residential unit in south London, to work alongside a multi-professional team of psychiatrists, educational psychologists, therapists, residential staff and teachers and to be responsible for finding new families for children who had suffered damage because of abuse or neglect. Just after I started, the Inner London Education Authority agreed to fund a classroom and a special needs teacher. My new role started as part-time but quickly became full time. Being a puffed-up newly qualified social worker full of jargon, I rang the unit and asked the officers in charge (we knew each other) if I could make an appointment to come and *"discuss my role"*. When I arrived on the appointed day, Bill Mercer, one of two officers in charge (his wife Brenda was the other) apologised that he could not see me for about half an hour because they were dealing with a visiting parent, so he took me out into the garden and introduced me to a six-year-old boy playing in the sandpit.

I sat down next to Geoffrey and tried to talk to him. He ignored me and carried on burying a toy car in the sand and then uncovering it. This went on for about half an hour with me failing to get a single word out of him. Bill Mercer came back and led me to the house and asked how I had got on and I said I hadn't got a word out of him. Bill responded by telling me that Geoffrey had been with them for six months and had not spoken, but his play had changed and from that it was possible to start to see some of what had happened to him. Bill had deliberately put me in that situation so that I grasped from the outset what an uphill task the centre struggled with. That was the point at which I decided to listen to what Bill and his wife had to say about the children rather than discuss "my role", leaving that for a time when I really understood the nature of the work being done.

Once I learnt to drop the jargon and began to learn about the individual children it was a fascinating journey, as all those youngsters I met would have been destined for long term residential care, because it would have been believed that new permanent families would have been unable to cope. Although I did not realise it until a couple of years later, no one was working in this way in 1972.

Working with other social work colleagues across the country we started to find families with whom a number of children were successfully placed. Two colleagues in Bristol, Pat Bellwood and Penny Hayward, came up with all kinds of families: childless couples, single people, older people whose children had grown up and "flown the nest", which encouraged us to think we could spread our net wider.

At the time the Children's Society employed a young press officer, Pam Chance, and I made an appointment to see her to discuss possible ways of recruiting families through publicity. Again, this was not happening elsewhere in the UK. I really had no idea how to do it or what safeguards needed to be built in. When I arrived at Pam's office for the first time she sort of blinked at me and said, *"I've never met a social worker before"*, this despite working in a social work organisation. At first, we were both very wary of each other. However, slowly but surely, we gained each other's confidence and Pam became very enthusiastic about the idea and came up with lots of creative possibilities.

Organisationally, the Society was well placed to deal with enquiries across England and Wales, but it would require the cooperation of local staff. This meant we had to persuade senior managers to back a national campaign that we hoped would not only benefit children at St Luke's but elsewhere as well. The deputy director Winifred Stone was enthusiastic and took on the task of persuading senior social workers in the various teams. All agreed to help, some, it has to be said, more enthusiastically than others because there was a lot of understandable anxiety about becoming involved with the media. They all knew me, but they did not know Pam Chance, because until now the social work division of the society had avoided her. Once everyone was on board it took another six months to plan the campaign as well as work out the systems to field and deal with enquiries from the public.

The campaign began with a press conference at which Winifred Stone invited Jane Rowe to speak. Jane was regarded as the most significant professional in the family placement field in the UK and USA at that time and a brilliant speaker. Would the press turn up? They did. Every national newspaper, some regional papers, some religious publications and a few magazines were there. We gave them written details to take away of children who needed families, as well as background information on the subject. It never occurred to us to provide photographs, but had we suggested it internally I doubt whether the campaign would have happened. Winifred, Jane and I all spoke and fielded questions. Jane was very relaxed and precise having had regular contact with the press, Winifred appeared calm but underneath I knew she was anxious. I was terrified and kept asking myself what on earth had possessed me to do this?

I needn't have worried; I think the press were as curious about us as we were about them. During the following days the national papers all produced major news reports and extensive features, the regional and religious press covered the story widely as did several magazines. Much more importantly, a lot of enquiries came in from the public and some children at St Luke's benefited as did others in various parts of England and Wales.

Afterwards, Pam Chance, who had previously been confined to fundraising duties, started to develop stories about the Society's social work and caring activities and she'd call me and say, "We have a request from this journalist or radio programme for an interview, would you do it?" So began my long ongoing contact with the media. Pam decided though that I needed to go on a media course which she found for me and would be filmed for her to look at afterwards. No pressure then! Afterwards she went through the video with me, pointing out where I could improve my presentation and it said a lot about our relationship that it worked so well. She also recorded every radio interview I did, helpfully noting and pointing out every piece of jargon that I used.

I had been out of college less than two years and I was on a steep learning curve, grappling with new placement concepts and approaches, (good to know Pam Chance did not eradicate all the jargon), coping with national organisational politics, facing and working with the media and working out systems to deal with enquiries from the public across the country and having them followed up. There was a risk, of course, of being sucked into the excitement of campaigns, but Bill and Brenda, Pam and Winifred continued to remind me why we were attempting these activities; to find families for children like Andrew, aged five, who had been beaten, neglected and locked in his bedroom for hours on end resulting in fear of the dark, and of adults (men in particular).

He did not know how to play and, because of the neglect, had to have a special diet that his underdeveloped tummy could cope with. And like eight-year-old Sian, who had been regularly sexually assaulted and tortured from the age of three resulting in terrible anxiety as a constant companion as well as physical damage from the assaults that could not be repaired, which in turn meant living with constant pain. Or Brian, aged eight and Afro-Caribbean, who was belittled by his white stepfather, scrubbed by him with bleach to make him white because, according to the stepfather, being black made him no better than the animals. He was constantly beaten and tied up to reinforce the point. And six-year-old Geoffrey, who I met playing in the sandpit.

All had been in a situation where saying anything about these experiences was impossible, fear dominating their thinking with memories well buried. Just to digress, not remembering or being willing or able to talk about abuse is a common experience for children. Fear is the most common reason for this, having had it drummed into them that something terrible will happen if they do. For many they will carry that fear well into adulthood, making sure it is well buried psychology. When journalists ask why they did not say something earlier, the answer is no one would believe them, they are afraid about what might happen if they do and burying the information is a way of surviving. Some will survive happily this way, others will not, coping perhaps with mental illness with little or no support. Sometimes it bubbles up to the surface later in life, triggered by something else and perhaps causing Post Traumatic Stress or full Post Traumatic Stress Disorder. In these cases, obtaining mental health services is difficult because some Trusts will argue that child abuse is not a mental health condition (which it is not). However, Post Traumatic Stress Disorder as an effect of child abuse, is a mental health condition.

For the children at St Luke's, the programme was intended to help them deal with the memory and effects of abuse, to move on and strengthen their resilience. Happily, they all found families who provided them with a very different, positive experience. Andrew subsequently had to cope with the loss of his adoptive father when he died suddenly, and we worried about whether his placement would fall apart. It didn't. He and his adoptive mother had a very strong emotional attachment and he grew up to become a car mechanic owning his own business.

Andrew also provided the best definition of a social worker I have ever heard. He was found playing in the garden one day by a member of staff and asked him what he was doing, and he replied, *"playing social workers"*. When asked what social workers did, he replied (remember I was his social worker) *"drink tea and play football"*. Best not to tell the *Daily Mail*.

Sian struggled with pain and anxiety in her new family but despite this found a career in nursing. Brian, who was very bright, settled well in an academic family, read law at university and is now a successful lawyer. Geoffrey, who had a very high IQ, found a feisty family who supported him through school difficulties and on to university, getting a first-class history degree and he is now in teaching.

In the early seventies my own family life underwent massive change. In August 1972 my dad died. He had had a serious accident at work two years earlier, smashing his right hand, and he never worked again. He was only sixty-one. He came from a family where few lived much beyond sixty because of a family history of heart disease, but I often felt he would have gone on a lot longer but for the accident; he just went too soon. In February the following year my mother died. She had been very dependent on and close to my father and when he died she tried to cope. When she got to Christmas I hoped we were turning a corner, but as soon as January arrived she went into decline. It wasn't so much depression in the clinical sense, more that the man who had meant so much to her had gone and she wanted to be with him. Mum took herself to bed and just did not get up and eventually pneumonia brought the end, aged fifty-three. I was just thirty and it felt as though my entire past had been cut out.

But 1973 was also the year my daughter was born and all the children at St Luke's wanted to see the new baby, so a visit was arranged. It was interesting to see their reactions. Most seemed frightened of the wriggling bundle but not Andrew. He asked what my daughter's name was and I explained it was Mairion, which was Welsh, and he repeated the pronunciation phonetically perfectly whereas adults in London just could not get it. He then said he had a present to give her, went off and brought her back his plastic hammer. We could have spent a lot of time analysing the gift but decided it was just an act of kindness and we wondered, given that kindness had not been part of his life prior to coming to St Luke's, where that gesture came from. Was it the experience at St Luke's or had just one person shown him some act of kindness in all the misery of the past? We just had to accept we would never know and be grateful that somewhere kindness had communicated itself and was positive. I just wished my mum and dad had lived long enough to see my daughter.

The Children's Society only had one office, its headquarters, and social workers worked from home. In 1974 the Society decided to set up one area office as an experiment, but the difficulty proved to be working out the size of an area. Because it was a national organisation there was a limit to how many offices they could set up. The first was to be based in East Grinstead in an outbuilding of a children's home and covering Sussex, Surrey and Kent. Winifred Stone asked to see me and suggested I set up this area office and become the Area Officer managing a social work team and six residential units. I knew nothing about managing a social work team or a residential service or setting up an office and it seemed rather alarming. Winifred assured me there would be a lot of support and was convinced I could do it.

The brief was not only to set up the office but bring together seven individuals into one social work team in order to develop their skills at placing children with special needs in permanent families, as well as reviewing the quality and future of the residential units. I concluded that if I was going to achieve this I was going to need some outside help as well as finding allies amongst the staff. Setting up the office was less alarming than I first thought: the building was there, the Society provided the furniture, equipment, stationery, telephone lines etc and I recruited the very good administrator, Avril.

Bringing the social work team together was another matter. Some welcomed the idea, others resisted, and none had any experience of placing children with special needs, but they did have a lot of experience of placing babies for adoption. Some did not accept the changing world of adoption. The peak for baby placement was the late sixties but after the advent of David Steele's Abortion Act in 1967 (3) and the development of the contraceptive pill, the birth rate rapidly declined, bringing a dramatic drop in the numbers of babies available for adoption. The emphasis was beginning to shift to older children, or those with disabilities, or groups of brothers and sisters, and so child care teams had to move with these changes.

However, bringing the team together was not helped by the fact that almost my very first act was to confront and subsequently sack one social worker for falsifying expenses and remaining at home when he should have been working. You can imagine the atmosphere at the next team meeting. Fortunately, most of the team knew what was going on, had been appalled but had not known what to do about it and somehow, with their help, we got through it. Over the next two years the same members of the team recruited a substantial number of new families for children with special needs and we started to offer those we could not use to the Adoption Resource Exchange, a charity operating a *"clearing house service"* for children and families waiting.

Reviewing the residential service across the area was an altogether different experience. I started reading a series of Home Office reports, some by Lucy Faithfull, one of their most formidable inspectors, from which it was clear she was not impressed with some of the units. There were four children's homes and two residential nurseries, and I decided to visit the children's homes first to get a sense of what they were like. In these circumstances you were inevitably invited to tea with the children, which was always eye opening; in the good children's homes teatime was a lively jokey occasion with incessant chatter around the table, whilst in those where there were concerns, there was a chill in the atmosphere and little talking amongst the children.

In one unit there was total silence at the tea table, and when I tried to talk to a child next to me I was glared at by the officer in charge. For a while the child did not answer but suddenly he did and was immediately shouted at to be quiet and taken out to the kitchen to eat on his own. As I left, the officer in charge said, "Do come again," to which I responded, "you will be hearing from me." I discussed the problems with my line manager who agreed we had to act, but we needed more ammunition and a plan for the future.

Shortly afterwards I chaired a review at the same home in respect of a five-year-old boy who had been excluded from primary school for disruptive behaviour. The residential staff were adamant that he was the worst behaved child they had ever come across, who took no notice of discipline. I adjourned the review so that I could see him for myself. He was whirling around a playroom bumping into things and sending them flying, and when anyone spoke to him he went around in ever tighter circles. Back at the review I asked where he sat in class and was told he was always put at the back out of the way, but he did not sit for long before he whirled around knocking furniture and other children over as if they were not there.

I tentatively asked if anyone had considered whether he could see properly, and the officer in charge of the unit snapped that of course he could see. The teacher, however, started to show some interest in my comment and so I suggested an ophthalmic assessment. Again, the officer in charge dismissed it so I told him that, whatever he thought, this child was going to have a full ophthalmic assessment even if I had to take him myself and the response, was "You do that, I am not going to waste my time." This man had got away with this approach for years and clearly thought he could continue.

An ophthalmic assessment was arranged with a carefully crafted letter sent to the hospital and two of my social work team took him. Apparently, he was chaotic in the consultation room but somehow all the tests were completed. The report showed he had only ten percent sight in one eye and 12.5 percent in the other. Effectively, he could not see, and the whirling around and bumping into things was about terror not disruptive behaviour. Winifred Stone and I decided to send two staff from another home the following day and get the officer in charge to my office at the same time. We went through the report and asked for his response, to which he replied, "It's rubbish." We informed him he was suspended and had to stay away from the unit pending an investigation. He laughed and said as soon as he had a word with the Society's director it would be we who were suspended, but he went pale when we told him the director had agreed the suspension. I called the director, something we had pre-arranged, and he confirmed to the officer in charge the suspension. We then set about closing the unit because the culture ran through the staff group. We found other placements for the children, with many of them going into new families including the boy with sight problems who subsequently thrived both in the family and at school.

We closed a second home for not dissimilar reasons; the so-called care was cold, critical and lacking any human compassion and a third because it was too isolated. It was located in beautiful woodland in Surrey, but local authorities did not like using it because of the isolation and the numbers were dwindling. The building was beautiful and the setting lovely and we thought it might be worth exploring the possibility of using it to offer holidays to families, predominantly single parent low-income families who could not afford them, as well as perhaps offering it to the new Intermediate Treatment Services for young offenders. After a great deal of consultation with local authorities and the local community, the holiday option for low income families and, a little later, Intermediate Treatment courses began, although we rationed the latter, because of the demand from families to experience a holiday for the first time, and we wanted them to come back again.

This left the problem of the two residential nurseries. I was not a fan of these places because I found the idea of rows and rows of cots with babies receiving only physical care inappropriate in 1975. In fact, as residential nurseries go, these were far better than the average because of the quality of the matrons who had already worked out that the future was more about supporting young parents to care for their children than about removing them, and in any case the birth rate was in decline. So, when I met with the staff I was pushing at an open door and they were ahead of me. Together we made a plan to put to Winifred Stone that would mean residential admissions would cease and there would be a transition into the provision of a *family centre*. In fact, it all happened very quickly. Winfred Stone was delighted with the plan and the staff were totally committed.

The matron and deputy in both units were lovely people who cared about very young parents instead of condemning and could see the difference good quality support could achieve. One of the matrons was liable to be quite stroppy if anyone was critical of young parents and suggested they should give up their baby for adoption. Years later I found out why, not from her but by watching a television programme about women's service during the war and she popped up as one of the women interviewed. In the interview she mentioned that as a very young woman she had had a baby *out of wedlock* (as it was described then), and her parents made her give the baby up for adoption and even now, in her seventies, she still thought about her daughter and hoped one day she would find her. I don't know whether she did find her daughter, but I know she, along with her deputy, was instrumental in so many young women being able to keep their babies when well-meaning but misguided people would have advised otherwise, and I feel privileged to have known them.

In 1976 my professional world was turned upside down by the Society's director Donald Bowie. He asked me to go to headquarters to meet him, which he had never done before, and it felt a bit like going into the headmaster's study, not knowing what I had done wrong. Donald was a lovely man and so enthusiastic about what we did, and I was very anxious about this appointment. When I went in he didn't seem angry, so I relaxed a bit. He was obviously struggling with how to have this conversation and followed a very circuitous route. He eventually got to a stage where he pointed out that he thought I had a lot of experience placing children with special needs, which was unusual. He then went on to ask if I had seen the advertisement for a new Director of the Adoption Resource Exchange (ARE) to replace Phyllida Sawbridge.

Phyllida, a bit like Jane Rowe, was a special needs adoption guru, so I began to suspect that for once Donald Bowie had taken leave of his senses. In response I pointed out that I did not have her academic background, her connections, had only qualified five years ago and was virtually unknown in the field, so they wouldn't even look at me. I remember him raising his eyebrows with exasperation as if to say what is wrong with this man. He tried again saying "even if you're right, there is no one else with your experience." I really thought he had lost it and maybe what he was really trying to say was that he wanted me to go and I asked him if this was the case. For the only time I can remember he was genuinely irritated with me and said something along the lines of "Of course I do not want to get rid of you, but it would be a feather in the Society's cap as well as yours." Before I could comment on it further he told me to go away, think about it and come back and give him my decision in the morning.

I went home, saw Donald the following morning and said no, I was not going to apply for the reasons discussed the previous day. "So be it," he said, "conversation ended." About a week later I got another call from him asking me to go and see him. Now I was getting exasperated. On arrival, Donald started all over again but much more directly this time and it was much more like a lecture on what I would do. It was so unlike him that I said I would think about it and he shook his head in disbelief. On the way out, I went to see Winifred Stone and asked her if she wanted me to leave. She looked totally perplexed, so I told her about my conversations with Donald and she stopped me and said, "You should apply, you know." So, I went through it all again, with Winifred shaking her head in disbelief. Eventually she said, "Stop under selling yourself and start thinking about what you have been doing and what people like Jane Rowe think about you." That confused me, as I had no idea what Jane thought about me. Winifred had another go, telling me I had nothing to lose. If I was not offered the post I wouldn't have lost anything and there would always be a job for me at the Children's Society, a comment that was to prove quite prophetic eight years down the line.

Having listened to Winifred I started to think differently and decided to apply on the basis that I had nothing to lose. To my surprise I was shortlisted and, prior to the interview with the other two applicants, had a chance to meet the senior staff to find out about each other. Amongst that staff group was a young woman who had qualified about the same time as me, called Liz Bowden, now my wife, though if anyone had suggested that twenty five years later we would meet again and get married we would have thought they were crazy. But we did meet again after my retirement and somehow our relationship changed and what would have been thought crazy twenty-five years earlier no longer seemed so.

Although I had applied on the basis of having nothing to lose, on the way to the interview I realised

I really wanted this job and thought that I would be extremely disappointed if I did not get it. The interview panel, chaired by Baroness Lucy Faithfull, the formidable former Home Office Inspector, did not make it easy. They were seated in front of a row of windows with the sun streaming in and facing me so that all I could see was a row of silhouettes. They offered me the post and after eleven and a half years I found myself leaving the organisation that had convinced me that my future was in social work and had nurtured that process.

Adoption Resource Exchange

A few weeks later my worst fears, which I had rehearsed with Donald Bowie, seemed to be about to be realised. Phyllida Sawbridge asked me to attend an event being run by the Exchange so she could introduce me to the members before she moved on. I was standing in the foyer with a coffee just beforehand when I overheard two people talking. One said to the other, "Do you know anything about this new director?". The reply was "Never heard of him," and they walked off. I experienced a sinking feeling as though those worst fears were about to become a reality, but I needn't have worried as the committee members, staff and the membership all gave me a warm welcome.

On my first morning, one of the staff, Murray Marks, a very able but outspoken man, put his head round my door and said the small professional staff group including him, Liz Bowden and Elizabeth Wilson had arranged to meet up for coffee at 10am and hoped I would join them, which I did. When I sat down Murray launched into one of his inimitable speeches, which informed me that all decisions in the organisation were made on a collegiate basis and the director most definitely did not make the decisions or direct operations. I probably said something like "I see" but thought "this is going to be interesting!". I had already made up my mind not to make any major changes in the first six months unless an event or circumstance occurred that required change. Because this was already a successful organisation and the staff had been so close to Phyllida, moving too quickly would de-stabilise the operation and Murray's statement seemed to confirm that my instincts were right.

However, in a small, dynamic organisation all sorts of changes occur speedily and organically in ways that are beyond your control. For example, within weeks of my arrival we were approached by Granada Television to see if we would be prepared to co-operate on a family-finding feature that currently went out in the North West but was going to go national. For us, it would mean designing a system to manage all the enquiries coming in, briefing our member agencies, fielding all the enquiries from the public and allocating them to agencies up and down the country to follow up and keeping track of progress. Our contact was a young woman, Ann de Stratford, with Liz Bowden our representative liaising with the television company, a formidable duo.

This was a controversial development. Granada's flagship programme *World in Action* had a year or two before made a one-off family-finding feature programme which both the Exchange and I had had a part in, but it had caused media waves. The nub of the controversy was whether or not it was right to show pictures on television of children who needed families. Some people disliked it, comparing it to selling cornflakes, others, like those of us at the Adoption Resource Exchange who were dealing with hundreds of requests for families for children with special needs, saw it as essential if we were to have any hope of meeting the demand.

Research evidence from the USA showed that people responded more positively to visual images than to the written word and were more likely to think more flexibly if they saw a picture. The controversy still bubbles along today, but we now have the negative complication to contend with of the risks of putting images on the internet. In 1977 we went ahead with the partnership with *Reports Action* for several series, and this was later joined by the BBC's Nationwide for two series.

Throughout the remainder of the 1970s the Exchange grew, with the number of children being placed doubling and we had opened several offices closer to local authorities and voluntary adoption agencies in Newcastle, Edinburgh (merging our activities north of the border within an existing Scottish Agency), Bristol and Cardiff with a regional office in London. This meant I spent quite a lot of time away from our London office to ensure the new structure worked effectively and regional staff did not feel isolated. In addition, we added Daphne Batty, Jenny Lord and Christine Hammond to our London-based staff.

When we had one office in London it was easy to keep a manual register of waiting children and waiting families using card systems such as Rolodex. With five offices it was a different matter. Computer systems were developing but because of their size, you needed a large room in which to house your own computer and in any case the cost was prohibitive. But an old school friend of mine, Colin Straker, now working in a large insurance company, told me about a scheme IBM had. They had vast computers and they would rent you space and provide access via a telephone line. There were issues of confidentiality to sort out but once we were satisfied, the company provided the service at half cost simply because they were fascinated by what we were trying to do. Basically, our staff entered information about waiting families and children into the system against a range of criteria and any one of our offices could access the details via a printer. Today we would think it very primitive but forty years ago it was state of the art.

In the latter half of 1977, the year my son Alun was born, the organisation arranged a conference with American adoption expert Kay Donley, who for many years had been running Spalding for Children, a very successful adoption agency in New York for children with special needs. One of the key features of the agency was to be honest that occasionally placements do not work out and when that happens you need to learn from the experience because by doing so, you can reduce the risks and help those at the centre of the case, including children and families, to cope.

I hate the public statements these days when politicians, managers and others claim: *"we have learnt the lessons"*, when you know perfectly well it's a good sound bite, and no one has learnt anything because the key people are excluded from any learning exercise. Kay's approach to learning what had caused a placement to come apart was to run what she called Disruption Meetings. The people attending these meetings were those directly involved, the professionals and managers with direct responsibility for the placement, the adoptive parents and sometimes an older child. Within the conference Kay described the detail of how the meeting worked by going through what was known about the child and family before placement, what emerged during the placement and, in the light of what was now known, what could have been done differently. A key component was that, although someone chaired the meeting, there was no "investigator" or attempt to blame, just a wish to understand.

Following the conference, we looked at how we could adapt what Kay was doing for a British setting and subsequently established a pattern where, when the placement of a child placed through the Exchange did not work out, we would convene a Disruption Meeting using a model based on Kay's work. Over time, as we gained experience, we were able to refine the model and produce a publication called Understanding Disruption (4), which underwent many reprints and updating, for other agencies to use. Although it's a long time since I worked in this field, I am told by people who do that this approach is still used so that the learning process can be ongoing.

In 1978 the BBC allowed us a fundraising slot on Radio 4. Colin Welland, who had just won an Oscar for the screenplay for *Chariots of Fire*, said he would record the appeal if I wrote the script. I was going to write a script for an Oscar-winning writer! I spent hours on it and sent it off to him, it came back with a note saying he had tweaked it a little. In fact, the only things left of my script were the name, address and telephone number of the organisation. The appeal raised a lot of money, helped in part by a woman walking into the office having heard it, and donating an antique Victorian watch but refusing to say who she was. We never did find out, and the watch was subsequently sold by Christie's Auction House for several thousand pounds.

It was a dynamic period in which so much was happening, and in 1979 I went to Houston to speak at an adoption conference and came across schemes called photo listing services that were increasing the placement possibilities for children.

The schemes were modelled on a system used by

American real estate offices. When people visited a real estate office they would be invited to look through a ring binder containing pictures and details of houses, making people narrow down their search before they had even looked at anything. The idea is that if someone sees the details of a house they like the look of, they might make an offer, even if it was above the price range they had in mind.

With the photo listing services, adoption agencies had ring binders with photos and details of children waiting, meaning that a family might consider a child outside of the group they thought they wanted. As with the use of television, a full assessment of the family's capacity to care would be necessary but this approach opened wider possibilities for children. Certainly, the statistics made impressive reading. On my return to the UK I discussed the possibility of launching a similar scheme, knowing we would have to go through the same debate we had over using pictures on television.

Outside the organisation there were mixed views, ranging from outright hostility through uncertainty to enthusiasm. To maximise the potential, we set up a planning group with representatives of agencies, adoptive parents groups and others and a scheme, called Be My Parent (5), was launched in April 1980. One local authority wrote us a very long letter before the launch explaining their objections. We negotiated and eventually they agreed to feature one child as an experiment.

We concluded that the child they referred was the most difficult they could find, on the assumption that he would not be placed. He was aged 14, had lived in residential care for many years with the likelihood he had been abused by his family and institutionalised. The first child placed was this lad. His new family was a large group with a mixture of birth children, foster children and adoptive children and parents, where the mother was in her late sixties and the father in his early seventies. If both the child and family had gone through a traditional placement route it is unlikely they would have been linked up, but it provided a powerful demonstration of how and why the scheme worked. The tabloid press dubbed it ordering children by mail order. The scheme continued until a few years ago, having placed many hundreds of children with special needs into long-term families.

During this period I was doing more media work, which had begun at the Children's Society. One morning I got a telephone call from a researcher at BBC Radio 2 about a story in the national press that morning about special needs adoption, mentioning the Adoption Resource Exchange and quoting me. They wanted me to be on that morning's Jimmy Young programme. It was a strange experience because my first knowledge of Jimmy Young was in the fifties when he was a pop singer with hits such as *Unchained Melody*. He turned out to be an incisive interviewer, even though he only had that morning's newspaper to go on. This was the beginning of a long-term relationship with the programme with me appearing on average once a month talking about adoption, fostering and general child care. This led to regular appearances on *You and Yours* on Radio 4 and even *Woman's Hour*.

Arrival of British Agencies for Adoption and Fostering

While the placement service continued to grow, behind the scenes change was on its way. At the end of the 1970s the UK was in a deep recession. Local authorities were strapped for cash (what's new?) and they were cutting back on funding for charities. Our sister organisation, the Association of British Adoption and Fostering Agencies (ABAFA) was negotiating with the Local Authority Associations for a substantial increase in its membership fees. At the same time, we were negotiating for a rise at inflation level for our charges. Out of the blue my opposite number at ABAFA and I were both summoned to a joint meeting by the local authority associations. We were informed that there would only be a substantial increase in subscriptions if the two organisations amalgamated. It was stressed that there was no room for negotiation, no merger, no increases.

This was a difficult situation. We could manage without an increase in membership fees because we had a substantial cushion of funding in our reserves, but our sister organisation did not and if they did not get the increase it would collapse. Just to make it worse, the government weighed in with the Department of Health threatening to withdraw grants to both organisations. If the threat was carried out both organisations would close. A lot of discussion took place inside both organisations with a lot of opposition to a merger, but eventually everyone accepted that we had no choice. Negotiations about the merger were difficult and it was the first time I had to stand on the side-lines while the two committees carried out their horse trading.

It was quite difficult to watch, our sister organisation saw itself as the "senior" organisation which, in terms of status, was true but financially it was in serious trouble and we were not, yet we came out of the deal with less. For me there were anxieties that I struggled with. Although I knew most of the staff in our sister organisation and in the main got on well with them, I was aware that in the enlarged staff group I would be the only non-graduate member of the professional staff of whom one or two had already made it clear I was not taken seriously.

The two committees agreed that my opposite number was to be the senior director and their chair would be the new chair. To placate me, it was suggested I too would have director in my title, so I became Director of Exchange Services. All sorts of positive things were said about how important I was to the new organisation, in particular I was a qualified social worker with practice and managerial experience in child care services whereas my colleague was a research academic, theoretically complementing each other. I knew deep down however, that was not how a small number of my new colleagues and trustees saw the situation.

There was disagreement over the name and the two sets of trustees were sent to a room and told they could not come out until they had agreed a new name. They say that when you design a thing by committee you will always end up with a camel and we got a camel; British Agencies for Adoption and Fostering (BAAF).

The merger took place on 1st October 1980 with a lot of positive noise and a large amount of metaphorical makeup to cover the cracks. Publicly all was sweetness and light; on the inside of the management team, it was anything but.

All sorts of incidents occurred, like a decision to cut my salary by ten percent without consulting me to create a differential between the senior director and myself. It was stopped by the vice-chair and treasurer, but it left a nasty taste in the mouth and damaged trust. On another occasion whilst away, my immediate staff were reassigned to other jobs, or moving my office to the other end of the building and as far away from my staff as possible.

After the merger I carried on my media activities, including regular radio appearances as before, which was giving the organisation publicity worth thousands of pounds for free. In 1983, however, I was told I should no longer accept media requests and to tell my contacts at the BBC that the senior director would be taking over all media interviews. Of course, media relationships need to be built, not taken over, and all my contacts were lost.

There were some supportive people around at this time, people like our treasurer Louis Hancock, our vice-chair, the late Madeline Carriline, two of our longstanding committee members, Ruth Hughes and Wendy Cann, Jane Rowe at the Department of Health as well as people like lawyer, Diana Rawstron. This was a new, challenging, and chastening experience, but one I would learn from. How visible the problems inside the organisation's management team were to other colleagues, I was never sure.

Whilst this was all going on there were also good things happening, such as teaching abroad. I spent six weeks lecturing in Australia, regularly lecturing in the USA through links with colleagues such as Mary Jane Fales in New York and Phyllis Tourse in Boston.

In 1978 Jane Rowe had suggested that Bill and Brenda Mercer from St Luke's and I should write up our experiences and turn them into a book and she offered to help with the editing. This was a challenge as there was not a writer between the three of us. We could write reports, but this was different. But we decided to try, which basically meant the three of us doing a lot of talking, me writing and my colleagues correcting. We started writing in 1978 and when we had got a manuscript together we gave it to Jane with much trepidation. Typically, Jane told us how good it was, only needing a few minor changes.

Jane was a very skilled writer and communicator

and her "minor" changes transformed it. She suggested we send it to Bill Jordan at Exeter University who was editing a social work series of books for publisher Basil Blackwell's in Oxford. It eventually came back with a note which, though it said some nice things, indicated that it did not fit with the rest of the series. We have no idea what happened next, but we got another letter a few months later to say he had changed his mind and *Building New Families Through Adoption and Fostering* (6) was published by Blackwell's late in 1982. Within BAAF there was animosity from some about the book as one or two thought it should have been offered to that organisation to publish but the objections were muted out of respect to Jane Rowe.

I was pleased for Bill and Brenda because it came right at the end of their careers and was a validation of the creative work they had done with some seriously damaged children and in the process taught me so much. Later, in the late nineties, when I went to Russia to do some consultancy work after the fall of communism, I met a young woman, Masha Ternouskia, who was on a mission to close all the huge institutions with upwards of a thousand beds. I was somewhat surprised to discover Masha had this book and was trying to replicate the work of St Luke's in Moscow, even though they had no similar culture of permanent family placement as we understood it. I suggested that, instead of trying to copy it, Masha should try to adapt it to the Russian culture. For example, I said, they had a form of guardianship that could be adapted and would be more readily understood by Russian people. When I saw her the following day Masha had a plan and a year later, had successfully set up and was running a new unit!

But life at BAAF was coming to an end for me. Having come back from holiday in August 1983

I found my job had been changed with most of my responsibilities dispersed and after a few days of thinking about this development, I decided to resign as I could not bear the thought of any more professional humiliation inside the organisation, whilst outside I was professionally respected. I had tried to put the organisation first when people advised me to stay for the sake of the agency and not respond to the experiences I was facing, but I now wondered if both the charity and I would have been better off had I moved on much earlier. Looking back now, there is an argument for saying I should have decided to only stay for twelve months but had I done so I would (though I did not know it at the time) have missed out on what was to come.

However, even at this stage I was asked not to talk to anyone about my decision, which I can only assume was because the organisation was trying to work out how to explain my resignation to the external professional world, but I was about to be overtaken by events.

The question I had to answer now was what on earth was I going to do? The fear of unemployment haunted me. However, I was not to know then that all my experiences, positive and negative, were going to stand me in good stead for what was coming next and I was to find I was going into a new role much stronger than I could have imagined.

Chapter 5 – Where Could I Go, What Could I do?

The child's unreasoning terror of being lost comes
as freshly on me now as it did then.
Charles Dickens, My Early Times
(The Folio Society, 1988)

A new challenge appeared and came from a piece of work that began in the late seventies. Sitting in my office at the Adoption Resource Exchange back then, Jane Rowe had persuaded me to help her put together a working group to see if we could bring a new project into being. Having tried to persuade some senior child care organisations to get involved she had only elicited limited interest. What had sparked Jane's concern to establish a new service was her leadership of a significant research project, the outcome of which was published as *Children Who Wait* (7). The closure of children's departments, with staff transferring into generic social services departments in the early seventies, caused Jane to become concerned at the loss of child care specialists and skills.

Her concern led to the idea of establishing an independent consultancy service to assist local authority staff to assess and cope with the most complex needs of children. In addition, there was a huge gap between the universal services such as education and health and the needs of children in the care system. From my earliest days at the Children's Society I had worked closely with child psychiatrists, educational and clinical psychologists, paediatricians, teachers and specialist lawyers, and understood what these professions could bring to make a difference, but it was also clear that the systems within which they worked sometimes got in the way.

From the late 1970s until 1984, Winifred Stone had been part of that group, which I had been chairing, consisting of some great people across a range of disciplines including Stephen Wolkind, one of the UK's leading child psychiatrists, Philip Edwards Senior Educational Psychologist who I had worked with at St Luke's, Diana Rawstron, one of the UK's most senior child and family lawyers, and of course Jane Rowe, to try and develop Jane's original idea.

In the early 1980s there was still a view pervading in education that nothing should be expected in terms of academic achievement for children looked after by the state, and you would hear statements like: "They are in care, what can you expect?" from people who should have known better. Child mental health services overall did not see children "in care" as being part of any service they delivered because the child was the responsibility of a local authority. It was also a time when black children in local authority care were subject to appalling racism, all of which, in combination, meant that children like these, whose experience to date was a mixture of neglect, abuse and loss were further disadvantaged by systems that were seriously flawed.

We struggled; the Department of Health said it was not needed, the Association of Directors of Social Services dismissed it as unnecessary as they had all the skills they needed. Yet the child care services were creaking under the weight of increasing numbers of children with greater needs coming into the system and no services for them.

It was Winifred Stone who came up with the

solution. The Children's Society would part-fund a demonstration project for three years, the rest of the money coming from charges to local authorities, but if it were to continue after that time it would have to be financially self-sufficient. To give the project the best chance of success, rather than have to build a complete organisation, the Society would employ the staff and provide the entire backup needed. It was an incredibly generous offer and The Bridge Child Care Consultancy Service was born.

Having resigned my post at BAAF, I was facing a future without a job, or so I thought. About a week after I had resigned Winifred Stone contacted me. By the summer of that year the Children's Society was ready to employ a director for the project and her call to me was to offer me the job. I was a bit concerned because this was Jane Rowe's idea and I was sure that she would want to run the project.

Winifred told me that it was Jane who had called her to say that I had resigned my job at BAAF and had not got another one to go to and suggested the post be offered to me (I had told Jane in advance of resigning that that was what I was going to do). It would mean a cut in salary and only a three-year contract, but because I had been working with Jane on the idea for so long and wanted to see it happen, I jumped at the chance. Once the Children's Society announced my new appointment the "cat was out of the bag". Therefore, in February 1984 a new journey into the unknown began.

Although I was at one level excited at the new challenge, which was something I passionately believed in, my confidence was at a low ebb feeling that I had failed in my previous post. During the first couple of weeks people like Ruth Hughes from Birmingham Social Services, Madeline Carriline, Louis Hancock from BAAF, Diana Rawstron and

Stephen Wolkind, called me to check I was OK. When I expressed my concerns about whether I was capable of doing the new job, they were all very positive and reminded me of the things I had achieved. Ruth commented "if anyone can make this work you can", whilst Madeline reminded me that both Winifred Stone and Jane Rowe were convinced that I could and would be on hand to help.

In addition, my new line manager was the Society's deputy director Ian Sparks who turned out, like so many people I had met in my career, to know instinctively how to support and get the best out of me and he was someone I came to respect and admire. At this point the new project, which didn't have a name, was given temporary office accommodation in a disused Christmas card warehouse in Camberwell while we looked for a more permanent base.

The Children's Society made their designer available to design stationery and publicity material, and it was he who came up with the name for the project. We had just located some office space, or so we thought, next to London Bridge, and he said that as we appeared to be about bridging gaps in all sorts of services why not call the project The Bridge. Once we added Child Care Consultancy Service to the name it made sense. Although the new offices did not materialise, we stuck with the name and in time found and secured offices next to Vauxhall Bridge. The name did change a few years later to The Bridge Child Care Development Service, when the word consultancy had become tainted. During the early eighties there had been a huge increase in the use of consultants by government as part of an outsourcing drive of services, another government initiative that was flawed because most of the individuals or groups commissioned knew little of the subject matter they dealt with, but cost millions.

An advisory working group, chaired by Baroness Lucy Faithfull (that formidable former Home Office Inspector) was set up to support the project and its members, drawn from the original working group, and included Jane Rowe, Stephen Wolkind (Consultant Child Psychiatrist), Philip Edwards (Senior Educational Psychologist), our lawyer Diana Rawstron, Social Work Lecturer, Maureen Stone, Robin Osmond, Director of Lambeth Social Services and a retired Consultant Paediatrician Basil Wolman. Because Baroness Faithfull had been Chair of the Adoption Resource Exchange I had got to know her and found that behind that formidable exterior was someone who cared deeply about children, young people and their families. Another endearing fact about her was that, although politically a Tory, she was forever being 'carpeted' by the Prime Minister Margaret Thatcher, for voting against her party in the Lords. It happened so often that I said to her one day, "Given your voting record, why don't you join either the Labour or Liberal party" and she replied, "My dear I could not do that, I was born a Tory! Every prime minister needs a thorn in their side".

The brief was to develop a service that could provide multi-disciplinary help to assess children's needs in a way that made sense to those dealing with the day-to-day care of particular children. Traditionally, where other services became involved as assessors, it was done in such a way that psychiatrists and others would assess the child themselves, produce a convoluted report, full of their own profession's jargon, which made little sense to anyone else. We wanted to turn that on its head.

Prior to setting up the project, the working group decided to try to test out our ideas with a supportive local authority (Wandsworth Social Services) and a social worker with a case she was struggling with. It proved an eye opener. Despite all our good intentions of developing a process that was much more accessible for those dealing with a child, we fell into the old traditional methods so ingrained in professional practice. As the social worker said at the end of the process, she was none the wiser afterwards than she had been before, the process left her outside the work and as she testily, and correctly, expressed it, the process was the same old methodology and of no help at all!

We were all somewhat chastened by the experience, but a model did emerge that was to change the way children's needs were assessed. The staff we appointed, included Gill Haworth, who was to be my deputy, and our new secretary Avril Cuthbert, all worked with our advisers, drawn from the original working group, to identify existing paper tools for collecting information in a factual and succinct way that could be adapted to our needs and design others to fill the gaps.

We also worked on establishing a process whereby the people at the centre of the case, social workers, teachers and others, used the paper tools to collect the factual information on a child but leaving out jargon and opinion (which probably made up to eighty per cent of the content of a child's file), enabling them to analyse, with our help, the collated information and draw conclusions on the fullest and most accurate information available. A lot of the children we were likely to meet had been around the system for some years and their files were thick and impenetrable with, in some cases, several volumes.

Amongst the paper tools we found elsewhere that we thought could be adapted to our purpose were health service growth charts, which, when used properly, could provide information about whether a child was following the pattern of growth that could be expected in relation to their birth measurements. Amongst the tools we designed were flow charts to record every move or change a child had in his or her life. These proved to be illuminating because so many of the children and young people we encountered had upwards of 20 moves of placement over a relatively short space of time. Most adults would find it challenging to cope with that, yet we expected vulnerable children to. When this information was matched with growth charts it became even more illuminating because, in almost every case, growth stopped or started in line with specific changes in the child's life.

We also designed observation charts to be used by staff seeing the child on a daily basis. At different times in the day a staff member would observe a child and write down what they saw, no opinion, and no 'I feel', 'I think' or any other extraneous information. This produced all sorts of interesting information about patterns of behaviour and whether there were specific things that triggered negative behaviour. When matched against information from the past and from growth charts, the pattern of the child's life became clearer. Many of these tools were to become widely used in Children's Services and the Department of Health published them in new guidance for professionals with responsibility for working with and caring for children and young people.

The model also provided for the project staff to act as coordinators, to show agency staff how to use the tools, chair the discussions that explored the information about a child and bring in specialist help when the local staff needed it, but not as a matter of course, and, above all, ensure the staff at the centre of a child's life analysed the information with our help so they could correctly understand it and make informed decisions. Over time, as our experience grew, the model would change but always remained faithful to the concept. Much more importantly the staff at the centre of the case grew in confidence in the methods and came to understand how to use the information in their possession and not feel confused or feel that external specialists were unhelpful.

With these building blocks in place, we undertook a major briefing drive for managers and staff of local authorities across the UK in preparation for the opening of the project on 1 October 1984.

Over the next three years The Bridge dealt with over seventy assessments using the model, and the research project following our programme, managed by Stephen Wolkind, Consultant Psychiatrist at the London Hospital, found that the outcomes for most were positive in terms of their lives, changing from a downward spiral of care with multiple placements to permanent long term stability, from multiple exclusions from school to making the most of the education available to them. But for some the starting point was so low that progress had to be measured in other ways.

The research showed that all had suffered some form of physical abuse, twenty-seven percent of young people had undetected or untreated health problems, twelve and a half percent had unrecognised special educational needs and fifteen percent had indicators giving rise to a suspicion or confirmation of sexual abuse.

One of the saddest young people we came across was a nineteen-year-old woman who had lived in mental health facilities (several in various parts of the country) since the age of three. At that time, she had been taken to see a child psychiatrist who was a friend of the family because her behaviour was "troublesome". The psychiatrist admitted the child to a psychiatric unit and advised she should remain in hospital long term even though there was no formal diagnosis of psychiatric illness, and the family were effectively told to go away and get on with their lives. An attempt to place her in the community at the age of 18 went badly wrong, and at that point the local authority came to us.

My deputy, Gill Haworth, coordinated the assessment and the bottom line was that there was no evidence of mental illness and the inappropriate psychiatric placements in various institutions between the south of England and Scotland had left her with learning difficulties and an emotional age of about three. The dilemma facing the local authority was 'what realistic plans could they make'. With the help of our educational psychologist, one of our psychiatric advisers and a clinical psychologist, the staff developed a programme of work designed to attempt to increase her emotional age and to try to give her a chance to relate more appropriately to adults. Alongside this, an educational programme was designed to match the age at which she was functioning, changing, we hoped, as she developed emotionally. To cut a very long story short, after 18 months another attempt was made to return her to the community but this time in sheltered care so that she was not trying to cope alone. It worked, and it was decided this would be her permanent home for as long as she wanted. The long-term damage caused by the crass decisions made when she was just three years old could not be completely undone but at least there was some hope of experiences that would give her a better life.

A very different story involved a ten-year-old boy who was regarded as disruptive in the children's home in which he lived. His behaviour was such that the residential unit were considering asking for him to be removed. As the assessment unfolded, a worrying picture emerged of a boy who had been ill-treated by his parents and other carers in two placements. Equally worryingly the history showed that he had lived in 23 different places in ten years.

When the changes were matched to the growth charts, his rate of growth diminished with each upheaval. It was, however, the observation charts that brought the causes of the boy's behaviour into sharp focus. Staff knew that the boy had experienced being locked in his room without light and beaten. He was also yet another black child who had his body scrubbed to make it "whiter".

In the current unit the observations showed that his behaviour was, for the most part, unremarkable, but there were three instances where a staff member wrote down what she had observed in relation to the way one member of staff treated him. This staff member walked into the room on each occasion and started baiting the boy with racial abuse, one comment recorded was that the boy should "be put down along with other black children". As the boy became agitated the staff member used more racist comments such as "you're a black animal" or "you are a f...... n.....and worth nothing". Eventually the boy hit out, at which point the officer in charge was sent for and the boy was taken and shut in his room.

This staff member's behaviour was a disgrace and mirrored the boy's early experience, so it was little wonder he hit out. What was equally worrying was that staff had reported similar incidents to managers who had taken no notice and, when confronted by the boy's behaviour, always blamed him. He was subsequently placed in a confident black foster family, where he thrived, whilst the staff member who carried out the abuse as well as **all** the managers were suspended pending a police investigation, following delivery of our report.

Subsequently, all were prosecuted and convicted, not for a race crime but cruelty. In my view they should have been prosecuted for both. Sadly, this case mirrored the state of race relations at the time and the appalling way in which so many children within the care system were treated, with staff behaviour condoned and covered up.

However, for one violent fifteen-year-old, before the assessment was completed he had carried out the random killing of a young woman and he was transferred to secure accommodation to await trial and his care and assessment transferred to the custodial services. He admitted his guilt but the assessment, with our support, showed he needed considerable psychiatric care and he was transferred to hospital.

As we continued the organisation's development we found ourselves involved in a new publication, Bruce's Story (8). Bruce was not a child but a fictional dog! At the beginning of the 1980s, when I was still at British Agencies for Adoption and Fostering, a colleague in our Edinburgh office, Maureen Thom, with another Scottish social worker, Celia Borland, showed me a story book that they had designed. Effectively, it was a family placement story but featuring a dog not a child. The text was just right for young children and the illustrations stunning. I suggested that we ask the publications manager to look at it and she was enthusiastic, but it was never published because of competing priorities in the publishing budget, as well as some opposition because it was about a dog not a child.

After I left to set up The Bridge, Maureen contacted me to ask if I had any ideas about who else might publish it and I asked her to send me another copy. In the meantime, I contacted the Director of BAAF to check they would not be publishing the book, which he confirmed, citing shortage of money. I contacted Mary Jean Pritchard at the Children's Society and showed it to her, and she too was enthusiastic. We met with Maureen and Celia to discuss the best way to publish and promote it. Its value was as a tool to be used by social workers and other professionals to help children understand the family placement process. We suggested adding worksheets with illustrations from the story that children could write or draw their thoughts on or even write to Bruce, which ultimately many of them did.

It really was a delightful book as well as a powerful story for helping children in the care system to focus on their future in a meaningful way. When published it went through several reprints and I still have my copy! Since then similar books have been published. The publishing manager Mary Jean Pritchard and her successor Emma Davidson were to become very important to the development of The Bridge.

This was a roller coaster period and in the 1980s I was asked to chair a government committee that was to dispense £4million in grants over three years to projects primarily to help single parents and children on low incomes. At the first meeting of the committee we discussed at length our concern that, because of the recession, local authorities were cutting grants to women's refuges which risked women being abused by partners, as there would be nowhere safe for them to go if they left. We decided to use twenty-five per cent of the funding to try to fill at least some of the gap. I mentioned our plan in a conversation with the then Secretary of State for Health, who was delighted to be able to give the Prime Minister some good news as that morning he had been given a rocket from the PM over something else he communicated.

A couple of hours later I was summoned to 10 Downing Street to be confronted by an angry Prime

Minister who did not like our decision at all and I was told, in a long tirade, to scrap the decision. The objections boiled down to the fact that there was no understanding of why women who were being beaten up by their partners did not leave. I tried in vain to get across why they could not leave, e.g. they were afraid that the partner would come after them and take the children or kill her, or the man controlled the money and the women could not see how they could cope without him and so on but with little sign that what I was saying was being understood. It is just possible that having lost control of the discussion, the Prime Minister was not able to engage in sensible conversation. However, it reached a stage where it was clear that the Prime Minister's mind just seemed to become closed.

I refused to back down and was sacked as the committee chair. On my way out I stopped and said, "of course I will be issuing a press release." and left. On the way back to the office I wished I had not been so rash as I would now have to draft a press release to get it to news agencies in time for the evening bulletins.

However, late in the afternoon the Secretary of State for Health called to say I had been "unsacked". He explained that the next person in to see the PM was the Deputy Prime Minister whose role was to "pour oil on troubled water" with the Prime Minister still angry. Apparently, he pointed out that fifty per cent of the electorate were women and if I issued the press release as threatened, stating the Prime Minister was not willing to help victims of domestic abuse, the next election could be lost. He went on to suggest that the Secretary of State for Health be instructed to telephone me and "unsack me". When our committee next met, I relayed all this and we agreed to implement our plan but increase the percentage we would give to refuges and therefore go further towards covering the cuts to refuge budgets.

As I write this, refuges for women suffering domestic abuse are again under threat. Successive government cuts to local authority funding means that councils are seeing refuges as an easy option for budget cuts and some of those organisations will close. Clearly in thirty years we have learnt very little and it is a disgrace because effectively government and councils are saying women who are the subject of abuse do not matter. How many more have to die before there is public outrage?

Another challenge was presented to us in 1987 by a computer-obsessed boy who sowed the seed for a later initiative. Computers had still not become commonplace in offices or in the home. We had two Apricots in the office and some families were starting to buy BBC computers, the first produced for home use to help children explore pre-designed educational programmes. The boy in question just could not or would not communicate with anyone, adults or children, but he spent hours in front of his BBC computer. All the professional staff at The Bridge and within the local authority felt totally inadequate. None of us could use a computer and it felt like a barrier between us and the child. We arranged for an art therapist to see him on the basis that his computer interest centred on the graphics within the programmes he was using, and it had some success and provided a means to slowly unlock his willingness to communicate but under protest. We wondered what we might have achieved if we could have communicated with him by computer. By the mid-nineties this was a theme we would return to.

By the beginning of 1987 the overriding question for us had become, 'can we turn The Bridge into a full independent charity?'. The Children's Society wanted to support us to do so, the local authorities with whom we had worked wanted us to try as did the staff and committee, and plans were made to launch the new charity on the 19th October 1987.

The organisation was now larger than in 1984 because of being awarded a grant in 1985 from the Department of Health, who two years previously had said we were not needed. This enabled us to increase the staff to appoint two new consultants, Sarah Jones and Aminah Sumpton plus two people, Penny Hayward and Pat Bellwood, to work on a part-time basis. In addition, we added researcher Marion Hundleby to the staff to set up a register of people who offered creative therapy, music, art, and dance across the UK and added Ann Bonney to our administrative staff. All the new professional staff had established senior careers in services for children and brought a breadth of knowledge and experience to the organisation. Over time we added more high quality social work professionals: Janet Lindsay German, Yvette Corte, Sheila Fitzpatrick, and Chris Fines.

By this time Baroness Faithfull had retired as chair and been replaced by Winifred Stone, and Louis Hancock, who had just retired, had joined us as our accountant and we were looking forward to an exciting future.

In the publicity material for the launch of the new charity Ian Sparks made the following insightful observation:

> *Manuals on personnel management are all agreed on the importance of induction for new staff, but none has useful advice on how to proceed when your opening line is "Now you are here, how do we make sure that both you and your project are completely independent of the organisation in three years' time?"*

We were about to find out.

Chapter 6 – *"It was the best of times and worst of times"*

Borrowed from Charles Dickens, A Tale of Two Cities

Then tragedy struck. To fit with new government guidance on child protection, Pat Bellwood and I had developed a new two-day child assessment course for professionals working with children who had suffered abuse and were looked after by local authorities. We were due to run the course for Berkshire Social Services on 15th and 16th October 1987. We were booked into a hotel in Windsor and on arrival on the evening of the 14th, as there were only two rooms left, and because Pat had more luggage than me, I suggested she have the larger of the two rooms on the top floor.

At around 6am on the 16th October, I was woken up by a terrific crash from somewhere in the building. I tried to ring reception but couldn't get a line, so I got up, dressed and went downstairs.

There was a lot of dust but no other sign of anything amiss. Outside wild winds were blowing, we were right in the middle of the 1987 hurricane. Staff told me that something had come adrift on the roof but there was nothing to worry about.

Because of flying glass at the rear, I decided to move my car around from the back of the hotel to the main street at the front. When I came back into the hotel I was met by the duty manager who told me that Pat was trapped in her room, but the rescue services were up there working to get her out though nobody seemed to know why she was trapped. I had to wait for two hours before the manager and a police officer came to tell me that the rescue services had reached Pat, but she was dead. Apparently at the height of the storm, the winds had blown over a chimney stack which had crashed through the roof and landed on Pat, killing her instantly.

The police interviewed me, asking lots of question about Pat and why we were there and then talked about telling Pat's family which I said I wanted to do. Reluctantly they agreed. I took a few minutes to compose myself, deciding not to try to wrap the message up in any way and just be precise and picked up the phone. Pat's family lived in Newcastle-upon-Tyne and when I spoke to her husband he was inevitably stunned, and I checked he had family locally he could call, which he had. I offered to make the call, but he wanted to do so, and I had to leave it at that. For Pat's husband and three children it was a terrible time and when I went to see them in Newcastle two days later, I hoped the fact that I could tell them I had seen her at the mortuary, that it was unlikely she knew anything of what happened and miraculously her face was unmarked might provide some small comfort. But really, I felt completely helpless, hopeless and guilty that I was alive.

I had known Pat for fifteen years and she was someone I admired and respected as a professional and a person. She brought a warmth and commitment to child care that was both compassionate and passionate. I count myself very lucky to have known her and just so sad that that time was cut short. Even today I ask myself could I have done more for the family?

Both myself and my colleagues felt her loss dreadfully but knew it was as nothing compared with what her family was going through. Even now thirty-one years later as I write this, the emotion of that time comes back causing me to shed tears.

The following Monday, 19th October, brought the launch of the new charity, now to be called The Bridge Child Care Development Service. The trustees had, over the weekend, taken over responsibility for its management because they knew how shattered staff were and all sorts of people who should not have been there turned up from across the country to support us when they had heard what had happened. They included an undersecretary at the Department of Health, Rupert Hughes, who absented himself from a very important departmental meeting to be with us. Rupert, a career civil servant, was, and continued to be, a great supporter of The Bridge and myself until I retired.

The process of recovery was slow, but it was helped by the support of all the specialists around us and the fact that in due time we asked Marion Hundleby (who had set up our therapy register) to join the team as one of our coordinators. Apart from her obvious skills, Marion was familiar with the organisation and had known Pat. In addition, we asked a brilliant trainer, Pat Curtis, to work with me on taking forward the training package that Pat Bellwood and I had developed.

By 1988, things were changing because many of the groups of staff we worked with were feeling much more confident in their own ability to deal with difficult cases, which was one of our aims, and we found ourselves providing more formal training programmes, and offering consultancy and advice to Family Centres. The same year brought the award of an OBE, which, as a committed republican, was difficult to accept. I did so in the end on the basis that small charities like The Bridge and their staff got very little recognition and this was a way of providing some. As one of my colleagues put it, OBE does not stand for Order of the British Empire but for "other buggers' efforts".

It was as a result of a piece of work in a Family Centre in Windsor led by a creative manager, Kathy Walsh, that we came across a game that had been developed by two of the centre's staff, Debbie Malone and Anne Jeffreys, called *The Needs Game* (9). It was a card game that was used with young parents to help them to identify what they thought the needs of their child were. The cards were very bright and colourful with images depicting a wide range of basic needs from food to love. What the staff found was that parents who found it difficult to answer if asked verbally what they thought their child's needs were, relaxed and could relate to the pictures in relation to their child. At one level it was a simple device, but it was this very simplicity that was so brilliant.

We suggested to the centre that this 'game' could be used elsewhere and asked, if we were able to find the money, could we publish it? In the centre, they used plain card and if one set became dog-eared then another one could be drawn. That would obviously not be practical for general use elsewhere, so we opted for laminated cards to prevent damage. We also included some blank laminated cards that could be written or drawn on by parents with a water-based pen if they thought there was a need that was not included in the existing cards and they could then be wiped clean afterwards. Together with the staff we wrote a set of instructions and then tested them out in a variety of settings. When *The Needs Game* was published, it got a lot of attention with the result that a large number were sold and used across the UK in Children's Services.

We used it in the assessment of parents too, although we were rather taken aback when a judge in a case in the family Court asked us to come and demonstrate it to her. The judge entered into the spirit of the game and insisted on playing the role of the parent. Given that when we had come across her before she had always been somewhat stern, the prospect of demonstrating the game to her, let alone having her play it, was rather daunting especially with the barristers in the case watching in a rather detached manner. The judge, however, while she was playing the game, drew the barristers in so that they, albeit reluctantly, joined in.

The point of this demonstration was that a local authority had used it as part of their assessment, and one barrister was very negative about it in court but could not describe it because he had never seen it. Rather than have endless legal arguments, the judge asked for the demonstration after which she was hooked. We heard subsequently that she was not above asking social workers if they had heard of *The Needs Game* and if they had not, sent them off to find one before the next hearing!

The Advent of Inquiries

In 1988 I received a telephone call that was to bring a major change of direction to The Bridge. The director of social services for a London Borough wanted us to carry out an inquiry into a foster care placement that went badly wrong. After discussing it with my colleagues I said no, because we felt we did not have the experience to run an inquiry. He accepted our decision but a few days later I got another call from him asking us to reconsider. He had contacted several organisations all of which declined. Again, I said no. A couple of weeks later I got a third call saying that, because of the quality of our work, he really wanted us to do this. I discussed it again with my colleagues and went back and said that we would take on the inquiry as long as the contract made it clear that we would be treating this as an experimental piece of work and that proved acceptable to him and his staff.

The question we first had to answer for ourselves was 'how do you run an inquiry?' There was no blueprint anywhere, and unlike our assessment model, this was an investigative role. After much discussion we concluded that assessment tools would lend themselves to the task and we should approach this inquiry without any wish to apportion blame, but to help professionals and the local authority learn from their experience and change practice.

In addition, we knew we could not run without the support of our advisers because we would be crossing interagency boundaries and specialisms. Therefore, there had to be detailed discussions with them all on process, which would include helping us to understand how the different disciplines work. We also needed to ensure we did not defame anyone when writing the final reports and we were particularly grateful to the legal advice given us by solicitor, Diana Rawstron and barrister, Mhairi McNab.

Child D

D's story at the centre of the first Inquiry we undertook was extraordinary. He had come our way because the foster home he had been living in, with very experienced foster parents, had inexplicably fallen apart with both carers developing serious psychiatric conditions and the child having to be removed aged thirteen.

We started by wading through the mountains of files and the story that emerged bore little resemblance to the summary we had been sent at the outset. D had been known to social services from a toddler onwards. His father was described as an alcoholic and his mother a heavy drinker, and both had suffered abuse and neglect as children.

Just after starting school, for reasons that were unclear, he was referred to the schools' psychological service for IQ testing. His overall IQ score was 125, above average. By the age of six there were major concerns about his welfare both at home and school and further psychological testing produced an overall IQ score showing it had dropped to 85. No one queried this, and he was sent away to boarding school for children with learning difficulties by the local education authority. Twelve months later his father, after a drinking binge, had a massive heart attack and died. D came home from boarding school for a week, but his mother forbade him to mention his father and he did not go to the funeral. A day later he returned to school.

A year further on, D was tested again, and his overall IQ was put at 65 and still this was not queried. This was a matter of serious concern because we cannot lose our IQ levels unless there is a serious blow to the head causing brain damage, brain disease or degenerative condition or severe trauma.

When D was eleven he went home for the summer holidays and his mother, like his father after a drinking binge, collapsed and died. It was D who called the ambulance and went with her to the hospital from where social services collected him and took him to a good residential unit.

D went back to school, but as time went by social services had introduced a new blanket policy that children should not live in residential care unless there was a clear specialist reason, foster care being the preferred option. Foster parents were to be required to help children make a life story book so that they could start to make sense of what had happened.to them. Sensible provisions in their way, but the trouble with blanket policies is that there are always exceptions to the rule, which proved to be the case for D.

He was moved to an experienced set of foster parents and everything went well at first until social services tried to enforce their "life story book" policy. At first the foster parents refused to cooperate, although there was no explanation why, and social workers thought this was out of character. However, pressure was applied to the foster carers and they were told if they did not comply they would no longer be able to foster. Because they liked being foster carers and they liked D, the carers gave in and tried to make a "life story book" with him but it quickly turned into a care disaster. Within a month it became clear that the carers were not coping and after two months a visiting social worker was appalled to find that the normally well-kept home was now filthy, excrement up the wall, foster carers and D dirty and unkempt. D was removed and that is where we came in.

Having pieced the story together in chronological order from the files we itemised a number of things that had gone wrong in D's life and were clear to see, some of which were beyond anyone's control, but others were the results of serious mistakes. But the key question was why did the foster carers lives disintegrate? The view within the team was that we also had to get to the bottom of the issue of D's IQ.

Our Educational Psychologist Adviser was clear that there was something very wrong with the range of test scores, so which were correct? We therefore started by arranging for our adviser to see D with the local psychologist, first by spending an hour with him playing football and then arranging to run several tests. The result was that in all the tests, his scores indicated an overall IQ figure of 125. The local psychologist, even though he was present, disputed the findings.

In the meantime, I arranged to see the foster carers, whose home was without doubt one of the filthiest homes I had ever visited, worse even than the description in the files. However, I spent two hours with the foster carers and went back for a second visit. It was eye opening.

In discussion the husband and wife opened up about their problems. To summarise, both had had traumatic childhoods which they had never talked about even to each other. The foster mother was four years of age when a German bomb fell on the street where she lived during the second world war, killing her parents, siblings and all her relatives, except one aunt. Today, some may find it odd that extended families all lived in the same street but back then it was not at all unusual. The only surviving relative, an aunt, brought her up and it was an era when the way of coping was to pick yourself up, dust yourself down and get on with life.

The foster father lost both his parents when a child because of illness and when he was thirteen his brother emigrated to Canada and they have never met since. The remainder of his childhood was spent with his only other living relative, an aunt. He too, just got on with his life.

They told me that when they were pressured by the local authority to make "a life story book" for D and they started to try to do this, the boy's story brought back all their own childhood traumas which had until now been successfully buried but now exploded into their consciousness. They could not cope, feeling that they were spiralling down into a pit of despair and depression. Although it was not a part of the Inquiry, we arranged for our psychiatric adviser to visit quickly and to organise urgent mental health services.

If you put the child's story alongside that of the

foster carers' it is, with the benefit of hindsight, possible to see how the placement fell apart. Could the local authority have worked this out? Only if someone independent of the placement could have spent the same amount of time with the family as we had without the pressures of expectations they had previously experienced.

A detailed discussion of the outcomes with the staff of the local authority immediately effected a change in relation to how policies on such things as the making of "life story books" and the development of a new rigorous procedure, to ensure inconsistent information such as IQ tests is dealt with and certainly the social work staff were appreciative of the outcome and made changes to their own practice.

However, there was still D's situation living in a special school with an educational psychologist who could not accept that the new test results for D were correct. A six-monthly review of D's case was due to be held at the school and the Director of Social Services asked me to attend to try and help sort out a plan for the boy and I agreed but only if everyone attending had a copy of our final report. I made the request because elected councillors wanted the report kept secret in case it got into the media and the council was publicly castigated. I had tried and failed to persuade them to hold a press conference and be open about it. However, the Director of Social Services did persuade them eventually to accept the report should be given to everyone who had a part in managing the case.

At the review it was clear social workers and teachers were interested in exploring the outcome, but not the educational psychologist. However, after a lengthy discussion with me insisting the boy should have the opportunity to participate, we worked out a plan that we hoped would help D's return to mainstream school and placement in a new family.

Because the Director of Social Services who had requested the Inquiry was delighted with the outcome, we found ourselves coping with an influx of requests to inquire into other cases where serious problems arose, including some horrendous child sex abuse cases. From 1989-1999 we carried out over fifty inquiries and serious case reviews.

Sukina

In 1990 we took on our first child death through abuse inquiry. Before this, our staff had worked singly with groups of mixed professions, but now we worked in teams of three, four, five and had to hone interviewing and forensic analysis skills as well as looking for speedier ways to make sense of the mountains of paper coming our way, dealing with the media, negotiating with senior managers and senior civil servants, writing and publishing detailed but accessible reports.

Publishing inquiry reports was another challenge. How could we ensure security of information during the publishing and printing process so there were no "leaks"? The answer was to find someone we could trust to manage publication security during the setting and printing process and that person turned out to be Ted Chapman. Ted fulfilled that role for sixteen years and I learnt a great deal about managing publishing tasks into the bargain.

It was another steep learning curve but the big advantage of having so many eminent multi-disciplinary professionals acting as advisers meant we had an extraordinary amount of expertise to draw on. We also had writing expertise to help us with reports, first from Mary Jean Pritchard and later from Emma

Davidson, both of whom were very skilled editors and made the publications much more accessible to a wider audience.

Sukina was aged five and lived in Bristol. The Department of Health had asked us to take on this piece of work, although with some managerial opposition locally.

When death visits a child because of illness or accident it is seen as a tragedy and can seem incomprehensible. All the more so when death is the result of murder or manslaughter by a stranger. Such tragedies become even more incomprehensible when the perpetrator is a parent or a carer, and people then look for someone to blame.

We were very aware that emotion and anguish are such that rational thought will go out of the window, and in its place will come media and political hysteria. In the aftermath of such events, trying to learn lessons whilst at the same time retaining sensitivity to the tragedy that has occurred is a difficult balancing act. One senior official at the then Department of Health and Social Security, when reading the Sukina report for the first time, became enraged at the description of the child's death in the preface. Below is the description we published in the final report (10):

The incident began with the father asking Sukina and her sister to spell their name, which they would not, or could not, do. When the request was repeated, both girls still did not respond. The father then hit Sukina on the hand repeatedly with a ruler, asking her to spell her name. Sukina still did not do so, but her younger sister spelled her own name.

Sukina never did spell her name as her father requested and, as each demand was not met with the response the father wanted, the attack escalated. She was beaten first with the ruler, then with a short length of rigid plastic tubing and finally with a length of kettle flex which had the kettle attachment at one end, but not the three-pin plug. We do not know how long the attack lasted, but at least fifty blows were rained upon her, interspersed with repeated demands that she spell her name. Sukina, at one stage, when she was too weak to stand, tried to crawl out of the room to the stairs, asking her father to stop hitting her.

Sukina's mother tried to intervene and was herself assaulted, causing injuries to her face which required hospital examination. The attack on Sukina continued until she was barely conscious, at which point she was taken by her parents to the bathroom and placed in a bath of warm water. At one point whilst lying in the bath, Sukina tried to lift herself from the lying position but was unable to do so. As she slipped into unconsciousness, Sukina told her father she was sorry. Although an ambulance was called, Sukina was dead on arrival at the hospital.

Apart from the pain of the attack itself, we can only speculate on the feelings of terror she must have experienced throughout the assault, but Sukina's apology to her father meant she, like so many abused children before her, was coping with the feeling that what had happened was her fault.

The civil servant explained it was too emotive and therefore the rest of the content was unacceptable. Killing a child *is* an emotive event which is something, in my view, we need to recognise. If reality is sanitised in the misguided belief that this will lead to "objectivity" then it will mean lessons can never be learnt. Acknowledging the emotiveness of such cases does not mean a loss of objectivity because, when added to stringent analysis, it enhances the ability to see reality.

Through other less traumatic inquiries, we had developed a number of paper tools and other means of managing information. In this Inquiry we used a paper-based chronology chart for the first time, through which we attempted to establish from a number of different agencies a clear chronology of events and their effect on the child, with key issues emerging as follows:

1. The father's use of fear to impose his will not just on the child but his partner and the professionals who tried to intervene. For example:

- terrorising a senior female staff member, when he knew she was on duty at the day nursery Sukina attended, by taking a Rottweiler into the building knowing the member of staff was afraid of dogs.

- Wrapping a pet boa constrictor around the neck of a new visiting health visitor.

- When social workers got too close to understanding the problems, making a complaint, sometimes of racism, to tie the system up for weeks and months at a time.

- Using physical violence against both his partner and child to terrorise them.

2. Staff feeling too afraid to complain to their managers about the way in which the father was attempting to terrorise them because they thought they would not be taken seriously.

3. Sukina's own views emerged from the chronology. One example was an occasion when Sukina complained of not feeling well at the day nursery and a staff member offered to take her home, but she said: *"please don't take me home, my father will beat **upon** me."* (emphasis is mine).

4. At the nursery Sukina complained about being hit at home but no marks were ever found.

5. The father was a member of a tae kwon do club and he had used his martial arts padded gloves to "beat upon" Sukina and the pain would have been excruciating.

6. Sukina was taken to different hospitals when she suffered a number of fractures, most of which could only have been caused by a twisting action, with the father relying on the hospitals not communicating with each other and thus remaining unaware of each incident.

This information was all contained in the files of seven agencies, 13 units and close to one hundred staff but had not been brought together because there was no system to enable that to happen, it is not very different today.

When a colleague and I interviewed the father in prison I asked him why he had beaten his wife and child and he replied: *"If my wife and children do not do what I want them to do, they have to be beaten to teach them to obey me, wouldn't you?"*

Violence against women and children is always about one person imposing their will on another and taking away their personal power. Unless we understand this we will never reduce the number of tragedies like this.

We were all very surprised when the Sukina report found its way onto many teaching reading lists including university courses for lawyers. One academic explained that it was because it was the first inquiry report to set out the facts in a chronology that only contained facts and was completely accessible to those not familiar with the subject.

Paul

The Inquiries kept coming and in 1995 we were asked to run an Inquiry into the death because of neglect of a 15-month-old child called Paul. It was an extraordinary case but was also the first Inquiry into the death of a child through neglect for 50 years since the death of Dennis O'Neil in 1945. It was not that children had not been dying of neglect, just that no one thought it important enough to ascertain why.

Paul was one of a large family group, with the eldest child aged 15, all of whom had suffered chronic neglect, although it had gone unrecognised. The chronology of events in the final report (11) showed several things:

- A basic assumption by professionals that neglect was caused by poverty, but no one noticed the adults, who were running all kinds of financial scams to convince professionals that if only their poverty and housing needs could be met they would be able to cope. Money from the various scams was rarely spent on the children.

- So entrenched were these beliefs that even after the child's death, the remaining professionals for the first few months were trying to return the children they had removed to the parents, even though the latter had been charged with offences that carried long prison sentences.

• Subsequently the eldest daughter became pregnant but felt unable to care for the child and placed it voluntarily into the care of a different authority. That authority, even though it had a copy of our report by this time, sought to place the child with Paul's mother when she came out of prison. As it happened our psychiatric adviser, who had helped us with the Inquiry, had been asked to assess the parenting capacity of Paul's mother and once she realised who she was, acted very quickly to prevent the plan going ahead. But it showed just how deep the confusion about causes of neglect run.

• That there was factual information going back years about the level of neglect contained in files across nine agencies, thirty units and upwards of one hundred staff including those working in health, social services, education, police, probation involved with the family, but it was never brought together in one place. This goes some way to explaining why it is so difficult for professionals to coordinate intense and complex information about long-term abuse and neglect.

We described Paul's death in our report as follows:

> *"Paul died on Sunday 7th March 1993. He had lain in urine-soaked bedding and clothes for a considerable number of days. Photographs taken after his death show burns over most of his body from the urine staining, plus septicaemia with septic lesions at the end of his*

fingers and toes. In addition, he was suffering from severe pneumonia. It is impossible to imagine the level of suffering that this little boy experienced as life slowly ebbed away".

In the preceding years there had been numerous reports on the other children in the family, scavenging in bins for food, coming to school hungry, the eldest girl trying to feed unsuitable food to Paul from bins because her mother was not feeding him. In addition, we found school staff had been providing food at school and taking food to the house.

The eldest girl, when her periods started, went to school with rags stuffed down her knickers and a staff member, when she noticed the problem, provided sanitary towels and went to the house to instruct the mother to ensure the teenager came to school with sanitary towels, something that never happened.

When the family moved into their current home it had just been refurbished but was now a tip with discarded tins, food, paper everywhere, the toilet had not worked for a very long time and there was excrement on the floor.

This list highlights the awfulness of the children's experience but also revealed the care and concern of teachers and others through genuine acts of kindness, which had however masked the real problems.

As the story of the case unfolded we realised we had to undertake extensive research into the definitions and causes of neglect if our report was to be of constructive use, because we needed to convey a message that would shift professional perceptions on the subject. We asked Wendy Alsop to undertake the task and she produced a clear, precise summary of the available good quality research which made it easier for us to explain what went wrong.

In trying to understand neglect we attempted to start from a perspective where we acknowledge that neglect can occur in wealthy as well as poor families and has little to do with available money. A Nigerian colleague once gave a telling account of the opposite of poverty leading to neglect:

> *"She told me about Red Cross feeding station one hundred miles north of Lagos where thousands of people were being provided with subsistence level rations to cope with famine. There, a mother who, having virtually run out of food, had walked over a hundred miles with her one-year-old child strapped to her back to reach a famine relief feeding station. During the journey the little food she had left she eked out for her child, eating nothing herself. On arrival at the station she was seriously ill, but she refused any help for herself until her child had been fed. "That," said my colleague, "is coping with poverty and it does not lead to neglect".*

Neglect is about the inability or unwillingness of adults to provide the basic needs of the children in their care: food, warmth, appropriate clothing, shelter, love and assistance with all the aspects of development. Their inability to parent is likely to be because they too had been neglected and abused or an unwillingness because their upbringing had failed them.

The effects of chronic neglect are greater in many ways than any other form of maltreatment; it is well documented in research studies from the mid-nineties onwards that long-term neglect causes severe impairment of: growth, intellectual development, emotional and psychological development. For example, research by Clausen and Crittenden (12);

Rosenberg and Cantwell (13); D. Skuse (14) spelled this out.

In this Inquiry those effects existed in all the surviving children, who were subject to long-term neglect, and the practical outcome when they reached adulthood would be that they would not know how to parent their own children and the cycle would begin again. If neglect is combined with exposure to violence or experiencing it directly and/or sexual abuse, the risk of the adult using savage violence on others increases.

Did our trawl through the research help overall? There is no doubt that, in the aftermath of the Paul Report, the number of children identified as being subjected to chronic neglect increased dramatically and, although there are still children occasionally dying because of neglect, many more are being removed before the range of damage listed above takes hold.

West Murders

The "Paul Inquiry" was quickly followed by The Bridge being asked to carry out a review into the role of agencies dealing with Heather and Charmaine West (15) killed by Fred and Rosemary West in and around Gloucester. This meant exploring the other ten murders which included the deaths of young people who had been in the care of Gloucestershire County Council and disappeared. In addition, we managed and participated in a massive tracing exercise with police and social services to try to find 2000 children who had spent time in children's homes in Gloucester over a thirty-year period. Not all the children were from Gloucester, they came from 42 other local authority areas as well. The purpose of the exercise was to establish if they were safe and well, whether they had any links with the Wests, and whether anything could be done to help them.

Trying to set up a process was testing, for a variety of reasons. Our investigation had to go back over thirty years, and the amount of paper we had to plough through was enormous. Finding the past staff who had met either Rosemary or Fred West was difficult enough, but tracing 2000 young people who had lived in children's homes over a 30-year period was something else, especially with the whole exercise being carried out under the gaze of the world's media, from whom there was constant pressure for information that we could not give. Whilst most journalists were sensible, a small number were manipulative or dishonest.

One day for example, I got a call from a journalist I vaguely knew who said he wanted to talk to me about my report into the West murders which he said he had read. I responded by saying: "What do you want to know?" He replied that he wanted to go through my conclusions, so I said, "Fire away." and he said, "Well, what are they?".

"If you have my report," I replied, "You will know what they are, and in fact you have not got my report have you?"

He continued to argue that he had until I said: "Well, that's all very interesting but you see you cannot have a copy of my report because I have not written it yet." At this point he accused me of misleading him and rang off!

A little later our offices in both London and Newbury were burgled on the same night, with the security alarms showing the same time. From the way the burglars searched it was obvious what they were looking for, and although the police came straight away there was no forensic evidence that pinpointed who was responsible, but you don't have to be clairvoyant to make an accurate guess about who was behind the burglaries. The burglars would have been disappointed in any case because we did not keep the West records at either address and neither did the computers have accessible information.

Although I think the police in Gloucester were understandably suspicious of our involvement at first, we quickly learnt how to work with them in a way that did not jeopardise their murder investigation. They also gave us access to a lot of data that would help us understand the scale of the horror in the case. Two of the saddest documents I have ever read were the statements given in court by two of the adult daughters of Fred West. The horror of what they went through and survived was indescribable.

The Wests' victims included: Fred West's first partner and baby, Heather and Charmaine, two of his daughters; vulnerable young people in the care system whom the Wests befriended; ordinary young women who happened to be in the wrong place at the wrong time and were randomly taken from the streets.

Their activities, it was clear, were completely indiscriminate, but the Wests' contact with agencies was limited. In the 1980s they were arrested, charged and convicted of a horrendous assault on a young woman and fined £50 by a magistrate, a sentence that beggared belief. The woman gave evidence again in the murder trial and the horror of the description of the original assault was stomach churning, even for hardened professionals.

When their daughters Charmaine and Heather stopped attending their school, teachers were told they had gone to live with relatives. They had in fact been tortured and murdered. At that time schools only had a responsibility to transfer school records if the receiving schools requested them. In the light of this case, the Department of Education, as it was then, implemented our recommendations to ensure that when a child moved, details of the new school were to be obtained, the records automatically passed to the new school and if the child did not appear, the local education authority had to be informed and it was their responsibility to trace the child. Unfortunately, this requirement has now been removed. Had it not been removed there would now be another avenue for locating children who are being trafficked. There is now evidence that traffickers are using care services and education to temporarily "park" children.

A local paediatrician visited the home by appointment and found all the children in different rooms involved in appropriate activities like practising the violin, or piano or playing board games, or reading. Investigations established that, as the family knew when the visit was to be made, the children were suitably "arranged" for the purpose.

The NSPCC had two contacts with the family but could not find their files.

Social services had two periods of contact in the late sixties and early nineties. The first set of contacts in the 1960s were unremarkable but those in the nineties were not. A girl approached a (very inexperienced) police constable in the street and alleged that one of her friends (the friend turned out to be one of the Wests' daughters) was being abused by her parents. The police officer reported this conversation to his station sergeant who immediately acted in concert with social services and investigated. The upshot was that the West children gave such graphic descriptions of abuse that should have been way outside their experience and they were removed, the Wests arrested and charged. In court the judge in the criminal proceedings threw the case out as he considered the evidence of the children to be fanciful.

The local authority immediately sought an emergency interim care order so as to retain the care of the children. In the full care hearing the court believed the children and a full care order was made. Considering that this all happened over twenty years ago it is remarkable that a young police constable acted so quickly, remarkable that the police and social services investigated and ensured, even when the Wests were acquitted of all charges, that they acted to retain the care of the children. But what happened next is even more remarkable.

In a foster home one of the children started talking about a sister no one knew about. The foster carer asked where the sister was and was told "under the patio". If the foster carer had thought to herself, 'this is stuff and nonsense', it would have been understandable, but she did not and instead called social services who in turn called the police. Again, it would have been understandable in the prevailing mood of the time, where what children in the care system said could not be trusted, if they had decided not to investigate. Instead they carefully interviewed the child who provided a name and roughly when it happened. The education authority was contacted to see if they had any record of this child and they did, noting that she had gone to live with relatives as had another a few years before. The Wests were interviewed and when attempts to trace the two girls failed, a decision was taken to dig up the patio and the rest, as they say, is history.

In our report we commended the police and social services for the actions taken, so often these professions are criticised for not acting and yet in this case, with so little to go on, they could not have been blamed if the people involved had not acted, after all one judge had already labelled the children's evidence unreliable.

Meantime, the task force trying to trace two thousand young people was beavering away and they found nineteen hundred and ninety-six, leaving four unaccounted for and there is no way of knowing what happened to them.

The media, which had been so keen to see our report, showed very little interest when it was published and the reason for this is summed up by a conversation that took place between two TV producers after the trial. I was waiting for the main press conference about the trial to finish, standing next to the two producers, who did not realise who I was. One said to the other:

> "Are you going to interview this guy Fitzgerald? The other replied: "No, can't be bothered, he isn't criticising anyone."

In a way it sums up what we know about some sections of the media; police and social services had done something very special including saving the lives of the surviving children, because if they had gone home they would undoubtedly have been next and the Wests would have been free to go on torturing and murdering.

In other words, some people in the media are only interested in those events where they can be critical of the police and social services but not when those services save lives. **The management of this case is the best example I have ever come across that demonstrates how critical it is that professionals must see and listen to children, suspend disbelief and develop an ability to think the unthinkable.** *However, it was apparently not worthy of publicising and a golden opportunity to educate professionals and public alike was lost.*

Other Inquiries or Opportunities to participate within Inquiries

The opposite was true and more typical in another piece of work where we were asked to provide a witness support programme for the North Wales Tribunal of Inquiry into Child Abuse. For several years there had been suggestions that there had been many cases of abuse in residential care and a series of investigations which found allegations to be credible, but decision makers chose not to believe them (and therefore the children were not believed) and the allegations swept under the carpet.

However, the allegations would not go away, repeatedly reappearing, and the social worker who had originally "blown the whistle" lost her job.

Demands for a Public Inquiry were growing through survivor groups and child care charities until the Secretary of State for Wales (pre-devolution) William Hague decided this had to be dealt with and set up a Public Inquiry chaired by Sir Ronald Waterhouse. I was very impressed by William Hague's decisiveness on this as he was genuinely appalled at what had been happening in residential care in North Wales. Previous Public Inquiries in other fields did not provide a witness support programme but the Zeebrugge Ferry Disaster Inquiry recommended this should be considered and the North Wales Inquiry was the first to attempt to put a programme in place to help survivors through the process, help them with reliving their experience in public and support them afterwards.

The Welsh Office approached several major child care and mental health organisations to invite them to provide this service, but all declined. Ultimately, they came to The Bridge Child Care Development Service and we realised we were a last resort but agreed. We had just six weeks in which to put the framework in place.

The team we used was a mixture of our own staff, and those seconded by other organisations such as Michelle Carlisle and freelance professionals like Sue Ferguson, Dave Herring and Joyce Brand. We added one of our consultants, Janet Lindsay German to the team and Wendy Alsop, to provide monthly sessions with staff to de-brief. We considered this to be necessary because they would be hearing horrific stories day after day outside of the inquiry hearings, then again when witnesses gave public evidence.

This was another steep learning curve because we would have to help witnesses who lived right across the UK including in some cases negotiating long-term mental health services, which was not straightforward when state services did not accept that abuse could trigger mental health problems. The witnesses carried the memory of traumatic events that had happened to them and were now reliving those experiences and there was a risk of, at the very least, post-traumatic stress occurring, a diagnosis that was only just starting to be understood more widely. Not only did we provide direct support to witnesses, we also found ourselves negotiating with mental health services where people needed additional help, trying to sort out housing problems and all sorts of other things we could not have anticipated. The full story was summarised as an appendix in the final Inquiry report (16).

It raised a lot of ethical questions in the way the review was conducted. Before we arrived on the scene, the ex-police officers employed to interview witnesses did so by turning up at their home without warning, which was causing a great deal of anxiety and stress because they were being asked to open up areas of their life that in many cases had been buried and closed down. Once we arrived we persuaded the tribunal chair to modify the procedure by insisting no one should be visited without an appointment, or making clear that they had the right not to be interviewed, be given information about our service and have one of our team sitting in on the interview, if this was what they would like. Of course it slowed down the process, but it made the needs of the adult witnesses central rather than peripheral to the tribunal process.

This was another experience that made us feel very privileged to have had this opportunity.

Another Inquiry where listening to young people was an issue involved two girls in residential care being exploited for sex. The Inquiry opened a dreadful story of girls of 12 and 13 being raped by two staff and sent off regularly in taxis to be raped by several men for money. Whilst the local authority and police investigated after a fashion, it was badly bungled, leaving the girls at the mercy of their abusers until we were asked to investigate. It was yet another case of children, for that is what they were, not being believed. Twenty years down the line it is still happening. The teenage girls were provided with a safe environment, but no staff were prosecuted and the Director of Social Services, who had been determined to uncover what was going on, lost his job because senior councillors said he should have "kept the lid on it", whilst the police were not prepared to discuss it.

I cannot say which of the inquiries and reviews I have managed was the worst, even allowing for the West murders. All have been horrific, and each child should not have their suffering or memory diminished as we try to present some form of professional exclusivity of experience. Below are three more descriptions of children's suffering. None died but the reader can make their own judgement as to whether one is worse than the other, or than any of the others I have described:

- *Child 1, aged five, was in her bedroom asking for milk and trying to get out; the doorway into child 3's bedroom was obstructed by three boards nailed across it, to a height of approximately 4feet 6 inches, and there was also a board nailed across the window; there was no bed, the mattress being on the floor with one blanket, and no carpet; the room smelled of urine. The bedroom was a downstairs lobby area, there was no light bulb. On examination there were various bruises and abrasions over her body and following X-rays, several broken bones were discovered.*

- *When the police visited a house, they found child 2, aged 14, tied to a banister naked and gagged. On admission to hospital a paediatrician examined child 2 and photographs of his injuries taken. These showed bruises and abrasions over the whole of his body, caused by the effects of chains and other instruments. Some of the abuse (such as being tied up for hours on end) had occurred over several weeks whilst other events, such as rape, happened over several years. The parents were prosecuted, and this was another case of the judge not believing the boy despite clear forensic evidence and dismissed the case. The Family Court, however, disagreed and made a Care Order to protect the teenager.*

- *Two girls were kept permanently upstairs, the staircase having been removed to ensure they could not escape. The eldest, 14, was repeatedly raped and tortured over a long period of time. Repeatedly, neighbours were reporting concerns to the Police, Health Visitors, Social Services, School Staff but their concerns were always rationalised as malicious. I met with six of the neighbours, they were not malicious but very concerned and if anyone had properly interviewed them it would have been difficult not to see their concern unless the interviewer was working with a closed mind.*

It was these same neighbours who alerted me to the fact that the father had conned the benefits agency into making a disability payment to his wife when she did not have a disability. The father had a number of scams and the family was not short of money. None of this money was spent on the children and the professionals dealing with the child care case were convinced the family were living in poverty; they were not. The parents had conned everybody except the neighbours.

These cases, like the earlier ones, are only the tip of the iceberg. Perhaps the reader can decide which is worse.

Working Internationally

From 1987 onwards, we also carried out a lot of work abroad. For example, I went to Australia in 1987 with a follow up visit in 1988 to assist a large charity that had a 1,000-bed hospital where children with physical disabilities spent their childhoods, many of them 2,000 miles from their families. The charity wanted to close this institution and provide services closer to the children's families, with the plan being driven by a dynamic senior social worker, Eva Leung. Unfortunately, many of the hospital staff were opposed and I was asked to work with them to look at how they could still contribute but in a very different way; a tall order. By the end of my second trip most staff had bought into the plan, with only a handful opposed.

On my two visits to Australia I met Brenton. He was 19 years old, suffering from muscular dystrophy and wheelchair bound. He had lived most of his life in hospital hundreds of miles away from his family and was very angry. Angry about not seeing his family, angry about spending all his life in hospital, angry about not being listened to and angry about being put into a wheelchair. Having read his medical notes and discussed them with one of our paediatric advisers, I felt he had every right to be angry about being put into a wheelchair when he was still a young child.

The mortality age for patients with muscular dystrophy in the eighties here in the UK was early 30s, whilst in Australia it was early 20s. In Australia at that time it was the practice to encourage wheelchair use at a much earlier age than it was in the UK, as it was thought it would give a child greater mobility, with the result that muscle wastage occurred faster, with the added problem of the lungs deteriorating more quickly.

Brenton was well aware that his life expectancy was very limited, which also fuelled his anger. His social worker was spending a lot of time trying to help him talk through his anger. I suggested the social worker treat it like a life story, start at the beginning and work through to the present and record the process so that Brenton had a record he could go back to anytime he wanted to. I also added that if he was willing to share his tapes with me, I would arrange for them to be transcribed and, if he would like me to, I would try to get them published as a small book.

Mary Jean Pritchard at the Children's Society responded positively and quickly to the idea and we set about transcribing the tapes when they arrived, editing and shaping the hard copy; not a quick process. We were just about to give it to the designer when I got a letter from Brenton's social worker to say he had died. Brenton wrote me a letter before he died to be sent after his death and wanted me to know that he was glad he had made the tapes, pleased they were to be turned into a book and although he would not see it he hoped it would help other young people in his situation. This was one of those moments when I shed a few tears, but I'm pleased to say that Brenton's Story (17) was published and sold in both Australia and the UK.

In the mid-nineties my new deputy, Renuka Jeyarajah Dent, made two trips to Estonia to help with mental health services. Both Renuka and I led a multi-disciplinary team in Russia to work with staff in residential institutions with upwards of 1000 beds, that was tough.

I felt privileged to serve as both President and Treasurer, at different times, of the European Forum of Child Welfare, an NGO which was an umbrella organisation for most of the major child care charities in Europe. Again, I met some amazingly committed people like Owen Keenan and Madeline Clarke from Ireland, Roberta Cecchetti from Italy, Marja Launis from Finland and Catriona Williams from Wales. In addition, the organisation was run by a remarkable young Belgian woman, Eleni Andrikopoulou, who seemed to have boundless energy, spoke so many languages, and could switch with ease between all of them in meetings. I went to Kosovo, with the

European Forum for Child Welfare, in the wake of the ethnic cleansing of an entire Muslim population, to look at therapeutic services in a situation where most of the population had suffered trauma. There I also met staff from a French agency who were very concerned about the political vacuum in Kosovo, because it was being used to traffic young women from countries like Ukraine and Moldova to western capitals.

On my return home I tried to interest the Department of Health, the Home Office and Foreign Office in the problem but I was told very firmly there was no such problem. The real reason for the lack of interest was, in part, that the Government would have been embarrassed had the problem been acknowledged when they were promoting their success in returning people to their homeland. I tried interesting the media but journalists would call the Ministry of Defence or Foreign Office to be told there were no problems so there was no one interested.

Today of course the trafficking of young women into the UK is causing political panic in the Home Office with estimates of 20,000 young women a year being brought here from many countries for the sex trade controlled by organised crime and bringing with it untold human suffering. When I read the press reports or watch the news I have repeatedly asked myself could I have done more to uncover this iniquitous trade; should I have done more? I regret that I seemed unable to.

Therapy Services for Children

By the early nineties my colleagues and I were becoming increasingly concerned about the lack of therapy facilities for children who had suffered abuse, especially outside London. Following discussions with several authorities we attempted to raise the funding for two therapy centres and were immensely grateful to BBC Children in Need, which provided enough grant money to carry out two experimental projects for three years.

The first was in Newbury with the enthusiastic support of Berkshire's Director of Social Services, Ann Parker and Assistant Director Margaret Sheather. Shortly afterwards we opened a second in Carmarthen, again with the support of two senior managers, David Halse in Pembrokeshire and Ann Williams in Carmarthen. In each project the local authority paid fees representing half the cost with the hope that if the centres were to continue they would be integrated into local services, either in social services or in child mental health services or both. Whilst one has become integrated into a local mental health service, generally we still face a situation, despite current government promises, of a very sparse provision.

Did it work? An evaluation exercise followed both projects and it became clear that the children being referred were those where every other option had been explored but failed, and therefore they were the children who presented the greatest difficulties. The art/play therapists in each centre provided weekly or two-weekly sessions for each child and over time each started to communicate, helping their carers and social workers to understand their disruptive behaviour. Then together they moved on to a more settled and hopeful future.

Among them was an eight-year-old girl who was totally out of control. Unless help could be found she was already heading towards secure accommodation. So difficult was she that when she came to the centre two staff came with her, and they and our staff had to stand by the external doors to stop her running out into the street. For that hour she was the centre of everyone's attention.

Slowly but surely the therapist gained her confidence and, together with the carers and social workers, worked to find ways to unlock her fears. Eventually the child revealed how she had been tied up by her step-father and locked in a cupboard for hours at a time without light, heat, food or drink. Everyone knew she had been beaten but this was new information. Gradually, through play and art, she worked through her story until the time arrived when no one had to stand by the doors to keep her in, she returned to school and did very well and then moved to a new permanent family, where she remained until going to university.

A second child, aged nine, was also providing control problems, but of a different kind. She would suddenly start screaming for ten minutes at a time for no apparent reason and repeat it throughout the day. Medical tests had not found anything that was causing pain and so our therapist was asked to see her. The screaming was certainly wearing! After several weeks coming to the centre, the child seemed to scream less but we had no idea why.

Then she started to reveal the most appalling details of her family life that no one had known. In summary her father over time impregnated her sisters and their friends and then performed abortions on them on the kitchen table. The child we were seeing was made to hold the knitting needles used and to watch the abortion being carried out. The police investigated and found the girl's story was true. The screaming was triggered by minor incidents which caused flashbacks to the dreadful memories. After a year, the screams had disappeared; she started a new school and moved into a new permanent family.

The total cost to the local authority was less

than £1,000 per child, while the cost of secure accommodation was at that time around £100,000 a year, with hospital or specialist care costing a similar amount. Unfortunately, we live in an age when public agency budgets are so rigidly controlled it's easier to spend £100,000 on one form of care when a cheaper and better option is available but has no budget to fund it. Is it any better today? No.

The current Theresa May government is promising increases in child mental health spending, but promises have been made before, and the money diverted elsewhere. Only time will tell whether promises will now come to fruition or be diverted again or lost in the excruciating Brexit debate.

At the same time as the therapy centres were being developed we returned to an issue that first caused us concern in 1987, when we became aware of the potential use of computers as part of a process of communicating with young people. I have to say I was no more computer literate than I had been five years earlier but there was a challenge waiting for us. We found some money and with Sarah Jones, one of our long-term consultants, assisted by Emma Davidson, driving the project forward we set about experimenting with graphics packages, which it must be said were not that user friendly, to see if we could produce something that could be useful to professionals and young people.

We asked Sarah to take charge of the experiment for several reasons: firstly, she had considerable skills and experience in working with young people and secondly, only a limited knowledge of computers and this was important because few social workers had any either. Emma's publishing background was to provide the creative element. Over two years they experimented and tested until a product emerged called *My Life in Words and Pictures* (18) that was easy to use, and the testing had demonstrated that it really opened communication possibilities for children and social workers and changed the power relationship because young people were much more confident about new technology compared with professionals.

Looking back now, it would seem primitive, so fast has been the development of technology. For example, the actual graphics package was on a floppy disk; I doubt whether anyone under 30 would know what a floppy disk was! Subsequently, we transferred the content to CD. Since then others have produced programmes in keeping with current developments and some have taken our package as their starting point. Hard to believe that at the time it was cutting edge!

Using Computers to Collate Multi-Agency Information

One of the major problems identified in **every** child death inquiry is the inability of professionals to extract detailed factual information from the different agency files and share it in a coherent way. This was not because of wilful professional ineptness, (as it is very often portrayed in the media and by politicians) but because, as indicated earlier, the sheer volume of material and the number of agencies and individuals were impossible to collate in any meaningful way.

Starting with the Sukina Inquiry we developed a paper model, but it was incredibly time consuming and cumbersome and it mirrored the problems faced by agencies and people from across the professions. We recommended in the report that the Department of Health should set up some pilot computer programmes to make the process more accessible. Their response? It was not necessary. Which only served to demonstrate how out of touch the government professional advisers were.

We therefore set about trying to find a way ourselves. With help from various people we developed a model, using Microsoft Word, which most agencies were using to a greater or lesser extent, whereby information from across agencies could be input into the programme in any order and then digitally sorted by date. We started to use it on inquiries, and it transformed our ability to isolate key information irrespective of which agency held it and, in the process, showed all the organisations how to use this.

However, we recognised that we were still in the infancy of development and in the Paul Inquiry, we made similar recommendations to those we had made in the Sukina Report, which this time the Department of Health ignored. Because the agencies at the centre of the Inquiry were keen to explore the concept, we decided to set up an inter-agency meeting to discuss a way forward and invited the Department of Health to send a representative, which they agreed to do.

What happened next was somewhat bizarre. The meeting started without the professional adviser from the Department of Health who arrived ten minutes late, did not make any form of greeting or apology but stood in the doorway and said, "this is a complete waste of time" and left. Everyone was, to use the vernacular, gobsmacked. We soldiered on but it was obvious, without the department, it was going to be an uphill struggle.

So why did the Government respond so negatively? Two possible reasons were that a) the Department had had its fingers burnt several times on computer initiatives in terms of cost and failure, and b) the idea was not theirs and government departments hate ideas coming from outside when clearly the centre of the universe is Westminster.

Shortly after this episode my new deputy Renuka had a meeting with Anthony Finklestein CBE, professor of computer studies at University College London and explained our dilemma. He was fascinated and agreed to provide the means within his university to develop a programme that could do all that we wanted and more and which would be easy for agencies to use, and he did. We then published a short guide called *Child Protection and the Computer Age* (19).

The Victoria Climbié Inquiry (20) chaired by Lord Laming, the former Chief Social Worker at the Department of Health when that organisation was saying no to us, called for a new computerised programme that could collate and chronologize inter-agency information. He would not, however, give any consideration to our programme, it had to be new. They could have had ours for very little but decided to spend what turned out to be £224 million on the development of such a programme plus ongoing running costs of £40 million which ultimately failed to deliver and was terminated in 2010.

Chapter 7 – Lessons Learned?

"Let us take things as we find them: let us not attempt to distort them into what they are not. True philosophy deals with facts. We cannot make facts. All our wishing cannot change them. We must use them."
Cardinal Newman, Oxford University Sermons

Throughout the years I and my colleagues were carrying out inquiries and serious case reviews, as well as assessments and development work, the emphasis was on learning lessons that could be assimilated by professionals working in child protection (safeguarding) rather than finding someone to blame. It is rare for one individual to be culpable. For example, if there are fifteen agencies involved that means at least 100 individual people all of whom have just one part of the task in completing the "jigsaw", these situations are highly complex. Today the phrase "we have learned the lessons" or "we must learn the lessons" drop from the lips of politicians, senior managers or policy makers with great regularity, usually accompanied by a look of what I describe as pseudo-sincerity. I no longer work in this area but as I see case after case unfold through the news media, I watch and listen in frustration as the lessons of the past are ignored.

Part of the problem is that any inquiry or serious case review may resonate with professionals at the time, but the lessons are not integrated into practice across all the professional agencies, or their staff leave and the knowledge goes with them. In addition, there are areas of understanding that are ignored for fear of inappropriate "labelling" and finally politics gets in the way.

Before I bring my story to a close I want to explore some of these problems as they were present when I and my colleagues were struggling to make sense of some of the most significant child protection cases that agencies have had to deal with, and the politics hampered us then as they do others today.

Changing Culture

There is a serious problem of making sure, when inquiries and case reviews report, that the agencies and individuals at the centre of a case take on board the lessons. We found that where organisations and people worked closely with us through an inquiry or case review, the lessons were taken on board by those at the centre of the case, but the difficulty came when trying to make the lessons more widely known and accepted. People not directly involved have their own problems to deal with and a specific child death does not directly impact on them. Whether or not the lessons can be learnt in one agency depends on the senior management wanting to own the lessons, but unfortunately that is not always the case and then there is little hope of progress. Multiply that by the number of agencies across the UK (120+) and you can see the size of the problem.

Then there is the matter of professional arrogance which can occur in any profession, in an individual or a group. I have always been very frustrated in the aftermath of an inquiry by how many professionals will make public statements about how the particular circumstances could not occur in their area or team or unit because they all work well together.

I have noticed this phrase "we are working well

together" crops up quite frequently, particularly where something has gone wrong. Working well together is not an objective. If we work with people we like from similar backgrounds we may enjoy working together but that does not mean what we are doing is necessarily effective, in fact there is every chance we are not because of "group think". That is our minds focus on what we agree on rather than factual evidence. Such an approach is a mixture of arrogance, wilful blindness and denial, which will ensure no one will learn anything.

Because so many inquiries and case reviews are today an exercise in blame and the varying quality of senior management teams it is hardly surprising that a main objective is to cover backs.

Too many public agencies operate within a culture of fear that emanates from managers who have no emotional understanding of what caring means and makes it very difficult for other staff, especially women, to raise legitimate concerns.

An example was a request to review the child care practice in a local authority area office, but the underlying agenda was concern about the way the office was managed by the three male managers. Two of our most senior and significant members of staff, both women, working directly to me carried the responsibility for the work. They carried out the review of child care practice in our normal way but when in the area office sat in the main open office, so they could observe the dynamics.

It became clear quickly the female staff found the environment intimidating as they were regularly subjected to sexual harassment, inappropriate touching such as groping, sexual suggestions made throughout the day and copies of the Sun newspaper's page 3 put up in front of a different desk each day. Female staff never left the office singly but in pairs or larger groups. Our team were not approached but their presence did not put the male managers off their stride in relation to harassing the rest of the staff.

When interviewed away from the office in a different building, as part of the child care practice review, the female staff were also asked by my colleagues about the sexual harassment they had noticed. Some were too frightened to discuss it, others opened up once they felt they could trust the professional reviewers. They then persuaded their colleagues to talk to my colleagues and we collected statements from all the female area office employees.

A meeting was then arranged with the Director of Social Services, which I also attended and shared our findings. The Director was appalled. To cut a long story short a date and time was agreed when we would arrange a meeting with the area staff away from the area office, whilst the senior management team would meet with the three male area managers to suspend them with immediate effect and the police ready to arrest them as soon as they left the building. Unfortunately, the area manager was tipped off and he left the country. We explained to the area staff what was happening, and we were then joined by the Director of Social Services who was very good and was very clear that, whatever happened, the male managers would not be returning, that a new "acting" female management team would be arriving the following day and officers were at that moment removing all the offensive material put up by the managers.

Over the years we came across many examples of a management style that at best was "bullying" and as we have seen recently this is still far too prevalent but changing an organisational culture can only occur if the commitment to do so comes from the top.

A Concept of Dangerousness

In the Sukina report we recommended that, given the danger that children like her lived with, there was a need to establish significant research about dangerousness in relation to child protection work. This went down like a lead balloon in central government!

Criminology has long recognised the existence of dangerousness as a concept, but in child protection it produces an extraordinarily polarised debate. Professionals, journalists and politicians have objected on the grounds that it demonises people, claiming that solving poverty would mean that these problems would go away. What gets lost in such debates is that thinking in these terms will apply to a very small percentage of carers. Over ninety percent of families referred to social services are dealing with children in need for whom support systems are needed and not classified as dangerous. The difficulty is that dangerous carers present themselves as "being in need" and what was missing from our "tool kit" was a means of sorting out the differences between the two.

Other professionals, journalists and politicians think the concept is too weak, that people are evil. The word comes from religion, not from a process of understanding; if we do not understand, it must be evil. Look where the word got us when George W Bush and Tony Blair declared an axis of evil (a declaration made in our name without our permission) and the UK and USA became responsible for thousands of deaths in places like Iraq.

We were trying to understand the difference between the child who is in need and the child who is in danger and whose need is safety. With grant funding my deputy Renuka set up and managed a major project to search the existing research data and then to develop a tool that would help us predict what characteristics noted in carers should alert professionals to the **possibility** of the existence of a state of dangerousness for children and enable the design of a training package. The research was carried out by Ann Hagel from the Policy Studies Institute (21), who had an established reputation in criminology and was keen to be involved in the whole process. We could not have run the project without Ann: she was brilliant because she was able, and willing, to move between her specialism and ours. Once we had the research results we designed a tool, BridgeALERT (22), tested it with several local authority areas, and designed and tested a training package. The project material was published in 1998 and was very much Renuka's "baby" and the last part of the package was a practice guide *Dangerous Care: Working to protect children* (23).

The response from a senior professional adviser at the Department of Health was effusive about the quality of the research but damning about everything else. This is so typical of government. Politicians and civil servants bang on about "evidence-based practice", as long, that is, as you do not apply the evidence. There is a mountain of research within government on children's services issues, the results of which have never been applied to practice. Heaven forbid we should change anything for the better. In this country improvements in the lives of people come not from government departments but from the thousands of people who carry on regardless and make the changes needed. That's what we did. The outcome of the Dangerous Care project was picked up by professionals and agencies across the country, and researchers in Europe who were dealing with dangerous situations day in and day out, dangers that are sometimes directed at them.

Can dangerousness be predicted? Not in every case (and I would never suggest we can) but awareness can be heightened which can reduce risk. Let's look at this logically. If a child is allowed to walk down the middle of a motorway, they would be in danger and their circumstances could be described as in a state of dangerousness. Would there be an extended debate about the concept of dangerousness? Of course not. It's clear, it is unarguable. For a child who is in danger at home it is not considered as clear, but the outcome could be as serious. For a state of potential dangerousness to exist in a family's home, the research project showed that a cluster of the following indicators must exist:

- Evidence of carers who themselves experienced both violence **and** neglect in the home as children. Where violence exists, some form of neglect, physical or emotional, or both, inevitably exists. It is this combination that is critical because the violence keeps the child cowed, living in fear, whilst the neglect prevents normal emotional and intellectual development which in turn stops the child from learning how to cope with what life delivers. Therefore, the child grows into a carer who knows no different and with each generation the risks are ratcheted up until not only injuries occur but a high risk of death as well.

- Evidence that the child has direct experience of, or has been exposed to, violence and neglect in the home. This is the repeat of the carers' own experience as children but is likely to be more savage.

- Evidence of injuries and/or neglect in relation to the child or siblings. In child protection cases injuries rarely occur in isolation, there is a pattern. Neglect is not a one-off experience but an accumulation of experience that is never-ending and grinds the child down, coupled with a cold critical atmosphere in which to live.

• Evidence of children being so hungry they are scavenging in bins or asking adults other than their carers for food, never have new or clean clothes, are themselves dirty and smelly, have little in the way of bedding, or are kept in locked rooms without a toilet and washing facilities and teenage girls who are not prepared for the onset of menstruation and womanhood.

• Carers who have committed violent offences against their partners, children or members of the public.

• Carers who have a history of severe mental illness, where there is evidence of violence and non-compliance with their medication regime. *Can I stress this will only apply to a small number people who are experiencing mental illness, the vast majority of patients will not be in this category.*

• Carers who are defined as suffering from a personality disorder.

• Carers who believe using violence is an acceptable way of behaving.

At the time the Dangerous Care project was carried out the review of research results in relation to alcohol abuse, drug abuse and child protection was inconclusive in relation to indicators of dangerousness. However, since then numerous research projects have changed that perspective and long-term substance abuse where rehabilitation is not completed, particularly where this is repetitive, has been determined as an indicator of dangerousness.

Since the publication of the Dangerous Care material, other issues need to be added such as the prevalence of head injuries and the effect on the behaviour of the individual. For example, at the end of the nineties we carried out a review of the case of DM who had murdered a 12-year-old child, five months after leaving a residential treatment centre following abusing several children as a 14-year-old. There were many factors in the case, but it became clear from his history that as a child he had received many blows to the head and there had never been a neurological assessment. There is now considerable research in relation to the way accidental and sports head injuries can change individuals' behaviour including in some cases stimulating violence in a very small proportion of people, and it is something that needs to be taken equally seriously in relation to children who are beaten around the head. In DM's case we recommended that a neurological assessment should be carried out before release from prison and the Home Office purchased multiple copies of the report *Childhood Lost* (24) to circulate to those responsible for making decisions about his future. Whether that recommendation has been acted on I do not know.

It's not just in the care setting that dangerousness can be found but also in the professional world. If child protection services are not understanding the severity of a child's experience, then the level of danger for children increases. If some or all the indicators above exist but the professional services fail to see or interview a child, then this alone raises danger levels considerably.

Sometimes professionals are fobbed off by parents with spurious reasons why the child cannot be seen.

Fred and Rosemary West told schools two of their daughters had moved away when in fact they were under the patio. No one checked. A Serious Case Review Report in September 2013 about Daniel Pelka (25) commented that the reviewer could find no record of a conversation professionals had with the boy before he died as a result of torture and neglect.

And yet the Wests were brought down because police and social services **did listen to the children** in the family and the lives of surviving children were saved. If there is one single thing a professional can do to reduce risk it is to see the child, observe its condition (are there bruises, what are their living conditions like?), talk with the child and above all **listen to the child,** giving credence to their views by taking them into account when making a decision.

This is not a new idea. It has been hammered away at by numerous Inquiry Reports, by Serious Case Review Reports, research reports, groups supporting young people in the "looked after system" and reports from major charities working with children, such as Barnardo's and the Children's Society, not to mention the legally binding *UN Convention on the Rights of the Child* (26) and *still* children are not seen or communicated with in every case.

The reasons are mixed: failing to take the issue seriously, poor training, poor management because managers do not see it as a priority, leaving front line staff in a quandary, fiscal cuts resulting in front line staff not giving time to the task, at times poor practice, some professionals who simply do not know how to relate to young people or an unwillingness to think the unthinkable.

The challenge for professionals and managers is to ensure that every child they come into contact with is seen and listened to and, where manipulative parents prevent this by repeatedly giving dubious reasons for not doing so, then the risk of a state of dangerousness existing is high and action should be taken. It really is extraordinary that in 2018 someone long retired has to write this.

Another area where the task is very difficult to deal with is not bringing together or sharing all the factual information they hold about the child's and carers' histories. Every Inquiry or serious case review report has raised this as a critical failing. To recognise dangerousness, it is necessary to understand a child's and family's history because that is where the beginnings of problems can be found.

For example; if the police know that a carer has been convicted of X number of violent offences, irrespective of whether against adults in the home, children or strangers, that should ring "alarm bells" across all agencies. If it's coupled with a carer's own experience of violence as a child, the alarm bells should get louder.

If there are recorded incidents of domestic abuse, if the outcome is that the "abuser" retains control over the "victim" the volume of the "alarm bells" should be increasing.

If the child has had multiple serious injuries, then the alarm bells should get louder still and if neglect is a feature of a child's experience then the sound of the alarm bells should be deafening.

As I write this I have the report of the Pelka case (25) in front of me and just one example makes the point. Police visited the family thirty times in response to calls relating to domestic violence, but this was not communicated to the rest of the safeguarding system.

The reasons why failure is repeated are many but includes thick, disorganised files, in some cases several volumes, that are impenetrable, and would require more time to research than professionals have available. Then there are managers who do not understand the importance of linking history to current experience and develop policies that only focus on the here and now, thus tying professionals' hands.

Further professional difficulties occur when instead of accepting new evidence when it arrives, it is dismissed by rationalising away its significance. In one case a series of firearms convictions by a carer including wounding with intent were dismissed in a case conference as not significant because the offences were against other adults. Naïve.

When a safeguarding case is dealt with on a multi-agency basis, once the direction is set, changing it requires a major professional and managerial rethink, which may be perceived as losing face or a reluctance to have an open mind. Professor Eileen Munro found in a study published during the 1990s (27) that once the direction of a case is set in the first six weeks, it is unlikely to change, irrespective of the scale or nature of fresh evidence being brought to the decision-making process. Repeated community reports of serious abuse or neglect can also be treated as malicious without proper investigation. So often policy makers, managers and politicians are heard to say, "I do not want to look back, only forward." But if we are unaware of our history we will never understand the present. All of us are a product of our history.

A good example of this was evident in the Paul Inquiry (11): even though the boy had died because of appalling neglect, the local authority was planning to return the other children to the parents whilst they were awaiting trial. Those who had worked with the family over ten years saw the family as "dirty, smelly but happy"; an ethos which continued after Paul's death. The new evidence which failed to have an impact on decision making was the death of the child and charges related to causing Paul's death, evidence which could not have been more dramatic. The decision-making process only changed when the police, at a case conference, slid a collection of photographs along the table showing Paul's emaciated body, an action they were criticised for, but it was the thing that brought the professionals up short.

In the 1960s, American psychologist Irving J Janis (28) described this as "group think" which meant that a group, where the aim is consensus without looking at the evidence, risks losing objectivity because it is based on like-minded attitudes/opinions rather than factual evidence. Food for thought.

Put the indicators of dangerousness in families together with systems failures and a child's safety or otherwise risks being determined by luck. For readers not familiar with the subject it is important to understand that when material such as that contained in this chapter is set out clearly with benefit of hindsight, after years of study, it all looks clearer than it did at the time. But for staff working day to day with these cases the systems are inadequate, they lack time and resources to do the job properly and do not have the benefit of hindsight.

Despite all of my comments there is a need to understand that there is no way all child deaths caused by abuse or neglect can be prevented because there will always be carers who know how to manipulate the system and the professionals within it, in the same way the criminal fraternity escape detection. The best that can be achieved is to reduce the risks year on year, something that has not begun to be achieved even though government departments have tried to manipulate statistics, simply not collecting them for many years and, during the 1990s, losing at least three hundred serious case review reports.

Currently, the death rate from abuse or neglect is

stated by the Department of Education and Skills as averaging seventy per annum. However, the average figure only relates to England; when you add in Wales, Scotland and Northern Ireland the figure is upwards of one hundred and thirty. These are deaths at the hands of carers, contrasting dramatically with numbers of children being abducted and killed by strangers which averages six per annum.

In addition, Government Departments and Directors of Children Services are fond of saying the UK has fewer deaths through abuse or neglect than any other country. How do they know when there are no "like for like" statistics that we can compare? Some countries still do not keep statistics and indeed they were not kept systematically in the UK until 1999 and there is no uniformity across the world in terms of data collection. The reality is we have no idea how we compare. No doubt someone will want to argue that we have homicide conviction rates but as anyone who knows anything about that subject will tell us, conviction rates are misleading because there will be cases where no convictions occur. Some independent long-term research is desperately needed.

The lack of long-term longitudinal research has long hampered child protection work. If a professional works in medicine, he or she will be aware that there is ongoing research into serious conditions such as cancers. Such studies make small discoveries and raise more questions, which are picked up by the studies following along behind and so on over several decades. The point of this is a recognition that the medical condition and how it develops is complex and cannot be readily understood in one or two short small-scale studies; it is a long-term process with each year of study bringing fresh knowledge.

In child protection (safeguarding) this almost never happens. Except for a small handful of studies, most child protection research is small scale, "one off" and superficial, with nothing following along behind. One piece of research funded by the Department of Health involved interviews with a dozen families whose children had been removed by local authorities against their wishes. They were asked a series of questions about how they felt about that and how they viewed the service they had received from social workers. It was hardly a surprise when 98.5 percent said they felt angry and that the service they had received from social workers was useless. It would not have mattered, apart from the cost, had the government of the day not used that information to instruct social services to "soft pedal" in child protection cases. The sample was far too small, and the questions skewed so that the answers were quite predictable. I am not against asking parents for their views, but I am against research superficiality.

When speaking at a national conference to explore the lessons that could be learnt from the West Inquiries, I criticised the Department of Health for instructing local authorities to soft pedal on child protection knowing there were representatives of the department in the audience and not surprisingly they were unimpressed. So much so they took me to task over lunch, claiming no such instruction had been given. The discussion came to an abrupt end when I produced a copy of the letter to local authorities containing the instruction.

What is needed is ongoing research which, year on year, adds to professional knowledge of why some children are in dangerous situations and others are not, to stop institutional foolishness as above. Such research will help us to measure the protectiveness of carers, and establish how to ensure safety in our systems.

To summarise, if the risks to children and young people are to be reduced there is a need to systematically ensure that:

a)   Politicians and senior managers stop paying lip service to learning lessons and support professionals by making sure they have the right resources.

b)   Professionals understand there are children in need who require support and children in danger who need to be made safe. It is not about promoting one above the other.

c)   The right training is available and mandatory across disciplines for all professionals.

d)   The right integrated systems are in place to share information swiftly and effectively, so that social workers and others are not bogged down by administration.

e)   We put an end to a blame culture directed at professionals who are struggling with very difficult people. The people who cause the deaths of these children are those with the day to day care, not the professionals who are trying to solve the problems. I would be very interested to see what would happen if over-critical politicians or journalists were managing these situations.

f)   All professionals understand the significance of children and family histories in decision making.

g)   All professionals understand the part substance and alcohol abuse can play in creating risk for children and young people.

h)   All professionals understand the part severe and specific mental illness among a small number of patients, who have a history of violent behaviour and non-compliance with medication programmes, can play in creating risks for children and young people.

i)   Policy makers, politicians, professionals start to recognise there is a world of dangerousness inhabited by some children and cease denying its existence for ideological reasons.

j)   There is ongoing high-quality research that is geared to increasing our knowledge over time and avoids the superficiality of the past. David Cameron asked Professor Eileen Munro to take a long hard look at child protection and to produce a report (29) with significant recommendations. Professor Munro produced what is arguably the most significant report on the subject we have had for decades but how much has been implemented is another matter. The government might like to consider asking researchers such as Professor Munro (who is one of our most renowned and sensible research academics) and a leading research academic like Ann Hagel who has specialised in criminology and dangerousness research, to develop a ten-year research strategy focusing on the needs of children in danger of significant harm, with the funding to implement it. Anyone in government listening?

k)   Constant organisational reorganisation, which costs monumental amounts of money for little return other than demonstrating "someone is doing something", ceases. Reorganisations also place children at risk, as those who are being reorganised are coping with unnecessary change when they should be coping with the needs of children at risk.

l)   Above all ensure that **all children and young people in touch with safeguarding services are always seen, their views obtained and listened to.**

I would suggest that if those twelve points are implemented, potentially progress can be made to reduce the numbers of children dying because of abuse or neglect as well as possibly the numbers of children experiencing abuse. However, such an approach can only be effective if the whole of the child care system is functioning fully and integrates these lessons. For example, an end to cutting preventive services such as Sure Start which have been so effective in both preventing children going into care and providing safe care at home. It is no coincidence the numbers of Care Orders increase exponentially with the decrease in preventive services and will get worse if refuges close. In addition, we still do not have joined up services in which agencies at a managerial level such as social services, health, education, police and others have a responsibility to make the system work.

Lastly, eradicating poverty is in the best interests of children and families (and long overdue) as being poor does produce unacceptable pressures for people trying to care for children, but the new universal credit system is making the situation worse because of the methodology being used. However, in my experience, children are not murdered or sexually abused because of poverty. Therefore, I would suggest this is why it is necessary to think the unthinkable when trying to sort out which families are a danger to children from the ninety-five percent who are not, where parents do care but are struggling with the difficulties that life throws at them.

For most children, childhood is a time of developing and learning and I hope having childhood fun, but for a small yet significant number, childhood is an ongoing nightmare.

The Politics of Child Death and Protection

Are there any political aspects to child death and protection? Emphatically yes, though there may be those who find the idea that a political agenda might exist in relation to safeguarding children, distasteful or disturbing. To get a handle on where I am coming from a little bit more personal history is necessary.

Within six weeks of The Bridge launching its service we ran into politics and everything stopped with the receipt of a letter from the local government union, NALGO (which subsequently became part of UNISON). The letter informed us that its executive committee had resolved to embargo our work, claiming we were a privatised service whose profits were to be paid to shareholders and that members of all union branches were being instructed not to cooperate with us. Local authorities stopped talking to us "officially", unofficially there was a lot of contact including with NALGO members. With the help of my deputy Gill Haworth, who had arrived at The Bridge via being on a picket line in a dispute in Tower Hamlets, we wrote to NALGO stating the obvious – that it would be illegal for a charity to make a profit, to pay those profits to shareholders and, in any case, our service was geared to helping local authority staff do their job, not towards replacing them. NALGO members in various parts of the country were also writing in large numbers in similar vein to the union's head office.

After a couple of weeks, a senior union official

called to ask for a meeting. When he arrived he looked very uncomfortable, basically waffled and went away. Another two weeks and another letter. This time the union stated that they had withdrawn the embargo! As life returned to normal we resisted the temptation to put NALGO Approved on the bottom of our letterhead as the whole episode had led to our position within local authorities being considerably strengthened.

However, most aspects of life, education, health, law and order, are subject to a political agenda and indeed elections are won or lost depending upon the ability of politicians to convince the electorate that "their way is the best way" to handle these matters. Indeed, it is suggested that talking tough on law and order or immigration can influence the outcomes of general elections; think Brexit.

Organisations operating in the private, charity or public sectors generally have their share of political games-playing that can have a serious effect on organisational functioning. Despite the fine rhetoric that can be heard from time to time about the wonders of our civil service, political (with a small p) games-playing by some civil servants and politicians has been turned into an art form, which the television series *Yes Minister* did not exaggerate.

Protecting (safeguarding) children and young people from harm, as opposed to public protection, is unlikely to have any impact upon the outcome of elections (after all children cannot vote) but the political games-playing that bedevils so many aspects of public life occurs just the same.

When I first became involved in Inquiries and Serious Case Reviews I could never understand why a particular case was selected to be the subject of an Inquiry and then hit the media headlines when so many other equally serious situations did not. It is only with the passage of time that we may be able to see the patterns emerging.

For example: the Curtis Committee 1946 (30) investigation into the death of Dennis O'Neil who had been evacuated from London during the second world war under a government scheme to move children away from the bombing in cities to the country, and his death was potentially an embarrassment for the government of the day. Coincidence? Or, Maria Colwell, aged seven, in 1973. The Labour government of the day was at loggerheads with a true-blue Tory Council (31). Social Services had only just come into being replacing the Children's Department. Coincidence?

Or Jasmine Beckford, aged four in 1984, killed by her step-father. The case was being handled by Brent Social Services, at that time a fairly strident Labour Council, which was locked into a bitter dispute with the Thatcher government over local authority spending (32). Coincidence?

The list gets longer: Tyra Henry, aged 22 months, in 1984, killed by her father. The case was being handled by Lambeth Social Services (33), another left-wing Labour Council and, as with Brent, locked into a dispute with the Thatcher government over local spending. Coincidence? Or Sukina, aged five, 1989, killed by her father in Bristol. The sitting MP for the constituency in which Sukina died (also part of a left-wing local authority in conflict with the Thatcher government) was the then Tory Secretary of State for Health. Coincidence?

And more. Paul, aged 15 months, 1994, Islington. Another very left-wing labour local authority at loggerheads with the Major Government. Coincidence? Rikki Neave aged six, 1994. Cambridgeshire. This is a particularly odd one because although Rikki died no one was convicted of his murder or manslaughter, only his mother convicted of cruelty. Department of

Health Officials ordered the local authority to publish its own internal report, which ran counter to government guidance in *Working Together* and showed no interest in the Area Child Protection Committee Serious Case Review Report. During the course of his life Rikki and his mother had lived for a short time in the constituencies of the chairman of the Conservative Party and the then Prime Minister, John Major (34). Coincidence?

Then there is DM (24) aged 18, 2000. Bournemouth, Durham and Newcastle. This young man who, aged 14, having been convicted of 12 specimen sexual offences against children, was sent to a residential treatment centre and upon leaving murdered a child. The residential treatment centre was situated in the constituency of the then Prime Minister, Tony Blair. Coincidence?

Lastly the Victoria Climbié Inquiry (20) raises some interesting questions about why a public Inquiry was held into her death. It is true that she suffered terrible torture and a horrendous death but so did many of the other 130 who died in the same year. Could it be that it was because Victoria had come to this country from West Africa and the government wanted to avoid an international incident? Would the Inquiry have been held had she been born in Sheffield, Liverpool or Scunthorpe? Coincidence?

We will probably never know the full reasons why these children and not others became the subject of major inquiries, or whether the coincidences suggested above were just that. Common sense would suggest that coincidence alone cannot explain the phenomena. How much of the motivation to set up an inquiry would come from politicians and how much from civil servants anxious to cover the backs of their political masters we will never know.

What I do know is that in a large percentage of

the serious case reviews or inquiries that The Bridge has conducted we were repeatedly told that ministers and, in two cases, prime ministers, were taking a personal interest in particular cases and yet I only met a minister once to discuss the findings and she had only been appointed to that portfolio just before publication of the report. This suggests that the real driving force came from within the civil service or from political advisers.

The part played by a small minority of civil servants and political advisers is reinforced within inquiries and serious case reviews conducted by The Bridge, by the attempts made at various times to intervene inappropriately.

Just prior to publication of the Sukina report in 1991, we were instructed to remove all recommendations directed at central government. We refused. The result was that, while the report was at the printers, the Department of Health withdrew the funding promised to cover the cost of printing, leaving The Bridge with a £2000 bill (worth a great deal more today) and serious financial problems.

The stated reason for this action was that the report was "badly written". A consequence was that this was the first inquiry report to be sold rather than given to agencies and when it went out of print 10 years later sales had exceeded 5000 copies. Whilst the Social Services Inspectorate thought it was badly written the feedback we received from those buying copies was that it was, unlike other inquiry reports, very easy to read and provided practical solutions to intractable problems, which explains why the report still appears on training booklists and photocopies are still requested from time to time. So, was it perceived as badly written because we criticised the government or because it made sense and it caused the government embarrassment?

If that was not enough, some weeks after publication of the report, the core funding grant to The Bridge by the Department of Health was withdrawn with very little notice. Coincidence? We were forced to make two thirds of our staff redundant, which was a difficult and painful decision for those it directly affected, and those who remained. By this time Diana Rawstron had become our chair and I was extremely grateful that her wise counsel and that of our accountant Louis Hancock was available to me as the organisation attempted to weather some very "stormy waters".

Two weeks prior to the publication of another report, a Social Services Inspector wrote a lengthy letter to the chair of an Area Child Protection Committee (pre-cursor to Safeguarding Panels) setting out his conclusion that, in a serious case review report written by The Bridge, there was an inaccurate statement. The statement to which the inspector referred made clear that health professionals had failed to share information as required by *"Working Together"* but that it was inaccurate because this guidance "whilst binding on local authorities had no statutory basis for health professionals". To suggest that *"Working Together"* was not legally binding on health professionals was at best "plain daft". Our response quickly resulted in the withdrawal of the complaint.

In another case a social services inspector contacted a member of a review panel who happened to be a manager in a social services department currently operating under Department of Health special measures and attempted to extract information about the review panel's deliberations. Now the government had been clear at the outset that the review had to be independent, and if at any time the lead inspector wanted information all they had to do was contact the chair of the review panel, in this case myself, and I would have provided information that it was appropriate to give, but it was not appropriate to put pressure on an individual who was in a vulnerable situation vis a vis the department. I made it clear that if further attempts were made to pressurise panel members in this way I would have no alternative but to issue a press release stating that the Department of Health had compromised the review and that a public inquiry would now be needed. Not surprisingly the individual concerned never accepted that they had acted inappropriately but did not intervene in that way again.

In the same case, just two weeks before the publication of the overview report, we received a telephone call from an inspector to say that the Home Office was unhappy about our comments relating to the use of the sex offenders register. A letter duly arrived from a section of the Home Office that had absolutely nothing to do with the issue or the case. We were particularly puzzled because the assertion that the report was inaccurate simply did not stand up to scrutiny. Because at that time the existence of the sex offenders register was new, we had contacted the Home Office for clarification before writing the report, and at each stage of drafting the report it had been scrutinised by three solicitors and a barrister. We therefore replied accordingly.

However, this only produced a bizarre response. The same person wrote, as he thought, to the various social services directors involved in the case to complain that the report was inaccurate and that I personally had refused to amend it! Unfortunately, he made two errors: one of the directors written to was not involved because some years earlier local government reorganisation had resulted in the case being taken over by a new authority (presumably the

Home Office records were not up to date). Secondly, given the high security surrounding the report, the letters were surprisingly not marked confidential so could be opened and read anywhere in those organisations.

The directors rightly passed the matter back to The Bridge, which wrote again reiterating our position but this time pointing out the above errors as well. On the morning of the press conference a letter was received by The Bridge from the Home Office, this time confirming the accuracy of the report (we had not changed a single word) and expressing concern that "because of miscommunication, the misunderstanding had arisen", a statement worthy of *Yes Minister*.

When the review carried out in relation to the West murders, to trace 2000 young people who had lived in residential care in Gloucestershire was complete, the report (35) was due to be published at a press conference. It was a report that contained 13 crucial recommendations for social services departments, the police and education. Two days before the press conference the Department of Health sent a briefing note to the then President of the Association of Social Service Directors telling him the report only affected residential units in Gloucestershire, ignoring the fact that many of the young people had been placed in Gloucestershire by 42 different local authorities. He appeared on the *Today* programme and condemned the report, killing the launch of the report stone dead.

Eighteen months later the Department of Health set up a residential care review in England led by Sir William Utting. I sent him a copy of the report referred to above and when he published his report (36) I was very surprised that he replicated our 13 recommendations and credited The Bridge. He added one recommendation of his own; that our recommendations should be implemented with a high degree of urgency. I had not considered I had that good a working relationship with him, but I have to say I was nothing but impressed by his objectivity and insistence.

Anxiety was probably the real cause of the examples of the behaviour outlined above, not on the part of ministers, but civil servants. Whilst such politicking in sensitive cases is not surprising, it adds to the pressure on those carrying out the inquiry or review and illustrates the importance of having high quality support and legal systems in place to survive the experience.

So much of the politics of child deaths are about blame or deflecting blame when what is needed is real understanding and just occasionally a government minister inappropriately enters the fray as they do in other areas. For example, whatever Ed Balls, the Labour Children's Services Minister at the time, thought (or anyone else thought) about the performance of Sharon Shoesmith, head of children's services in the Baby P case at the London Borough of Haringey, he had no right to stand up at a press conference and announce her dismissal when the process laid down in employment law (most of it enacted by Labour Governments) had not even started let alone been completed. That's not just my view but the view of the High Court:

> *October 2012 – High Court – ruled she had been "unfairly scapegoated" and that her removal from office by former Labour children's secretary, Ed Balls, was "intrinsically unfair and unlawful"*

It is not just in central government that these types of problems arise. For example other professions, such as lawyers (again in a small minority of cases), attempt to block progress inappropriately.

There was an attempt to prevent us from publishing another report because a Health Authority lawyer was advising that body it should not agree to publication. The reason given was that it would breach medical confidentiality. Letters from our lawyers and those of other agencies were flying about, but we could not "unstick" the problem until a meeting occurred with the health authority's lawyer and we discovered he had not read the report but was simply indulging in a knee jerk reaction. He was then instructed by his client (the health authority) to read the report and the meeting reconvened later in the day, at which point the report was pronounced publishable but with the lawyer setting about blaming The Bridge for the delay! We think he could see his fee disappearing!

In another case, The Bridge, the day before publication of an overview report, received what can only be described as a threatening fax from solicitors acting for a health trust, stating, amongst other things, that unless a written undertaking was given not to publish within the hour, an injunction would be obtained to prevent publication. A few telephone calls quickly ascertained that the health trust had not asked their solicitors to write but an individual acting without authority had done so. The Area Child Protection Committee and The Bridge simply replied, "See you in court", whilst the chief executive of the health trust instructed the solicitors to retract.

Another Area Child Protection Committee had been keen from the outset to publish the overview report. It approved the report and then, at the printers' proofs stage, panicked and wanted to re-write to dilute the contents. It took a lot of discussion to ensure that an accurate report was published.

Undoubtedly anxiety to escape criticism was the

motivation for the actions of the organisations and individuals in these examples and yet in most cases the more likely outcome was an opportunity to learn from the experience rather than be castigated by external forces such as the media.

Sometimes of course individuals' political games-playing can work in your favour, even if that was not the intention. After the withdrawal by the Department of Health of The Bridge's core funding, we went through a difficult time, but within eighteen months we were busier than ever, and we could not understand why. Some years later a deputy director of social services told me that when they asked the Department of Health for suggestions of who would be appropriate to carry out a high-profile inquiry, he and colleagues met with officials who gave them a list and discussed the pros and cons of each person on it. He told me that they got up to leave when the senior professional adviser in the department said, *"we probably ought to mention The Bridge Child Care Development Service, but you need to understand that the organisation and its Chief Executive, John Fitzgerald, are very difficult to work with".*

Outside, the group quickly concluded they would contact The Bridge because the way in which the information had been provided showed it was not in the government's pocket. It then transpired that this process had been played out many times before and most people had interpreted the statement in the same way and so our workload increased!

Other organisations, such as religious groups, also had difficulty coping with child abuse within their own ranks. The most extreme version, though not exclusively so, has been the behaviour of the Catholic Church. For decades priests (and nuns) who abused children were never reported to the police but simply moved to new parishes or orders that allowed them to go on behaving in the same way without fear of action being taken against them. There are signs that some religious groups are beginning to change. For example, Pope Francis, who had initially failed to act when child abuse by priests in the Catholic Church in Chile was alleged, when given the full information, demanded the resignation of all thirty of the country's bishops.

For the victims the message was clear, they were not considered important enough for their church to take the crimes against them seriously, that it did not care about the horrors visited upon them and often they were pressurised to stay quiet, all in the name of protecting the religion. It happened because the Catholic Church took a political decision to protect itself rather than deal with the needs of victims of horrific crimes.

But it was not just the Christian church that behaved in this way. Recently, a number of aid agencies were exposed as covering up child abuse and exploitation of women in disaster areas and in one case had no policies in place for dealing with such matters.

Given the behaviour of governments, religious institutions and others around the world, is it any wonder that there is confusion in society and professions trying to deal with child protection.

Political fallout can, however, be the result of sheer thoughtlessness. In 2003, after I retired, The Bridge merged with another charity and all its records were transferred into the new arrangement. In the early part of 2013 with a further inquiry into child abuse in North Wales being set up I approached that organisation to ask if I could access our old records but received the following response:

> *"The historic records relating to the work of The Bridge in this exercise were destroyed at*

the end of the required retention period as there was no basis for further retention for them. Therefore, I am not able to help you. We have no reason to make contact with the inquiry in Action for Children although of course we will co-operate fully with any questions raised by the team. There have been none raised with us to date."

It was subsequently confirmed that **all** of the records belonging to The Bridge Child Care Development Service had been destroyed under the organisation's blanket policy on storage and destruction of records. It takes a lot to shock me, but this did. The records held by The Bridge included more than one hundred on individual children that had been looked after by the state, which, under current legislation, should have been kept for 75 years. Therefore, those records which carried the extensive details of individual children's histories have been lost forever.

It sadly mirrors the institutional failures that ensure children are not at the centre of need when cared for by the state, that despite repeated inquiries lamenting the fact, organisations do not seem to understand the significance of children and family histories. In addition, the records relating to inquiries, such as the West murders, are a major slice of 20th century social history, which would have provided the basis for major academic research. The best one can say is that decisions were simply not thought through and should not have happened within an organisation that is one of the UK's major child care charities and professes to be acting in the interests of children to deal with abuse and neglect.

Fear of the media, however has driven many of the examples I've given. From the Maria Colwell

Inquiry onwards, some parts of media have been vitriolic in their criticism of professionals including social workers. The hacking scandal by journalists does nothing to soften my view. Anxiety, politics and manipulation, as in other walks of life, are all part of the process of dealing with child protection and it is naive to believe otherwise. When managing an inquiry or serious case review I have found I have spent as much time (and sometimes more) on sorting out these problems as I have on the inquiry or review process itself.

Most of all we are talking about professionalism and integrity. What is the difference between the abuser who beats and tortures his wife and children to impose his will, killing one of them, or a government exerting power through sexual harassment, or dropping bombs on countries that pose no direct threat to ours? Nothing. All set out to use force to impose their personal or political will, so it's hardly surprising if child death and protection becomes politicised.

Unfortunately, when it comes to learning lessons, too often our politicians and policy makers allow opinion to outweigh evidence and the good people in public service (the majority) fight an uphill and lengthy battle to be heard. In my view *every policy maker/politician,* should be forced to a) read Professor King's and Ivor Crew's book *Blunders of our Governments* (1) and b) sit an exam on the content. To pass, their answers must be eighty percent correct before they are selected or appointed.

This book has chapter after chapter of forensically researched blunders itemising foolish and financially costly schemes and projects by governments of all political backgrounds, as far back as 1945. The financial costs in terms of wasted money is eye watering, so much so that if all the money had been spent instead on the NHS, Education, Children's Services, Social Care, Pensions, a real living wage and student grants we would have long ago solved our economic problems in these areas and there would still be billions over to invest in our economy and job creation.

Chapter 8 - End of a career

*"I shot an arrow into the air. It fell to earth I
knew not where"*
Henry Wadsworth Longfellow 1807-1882

During my career I travelled a great deal and was
away from home a lot and coping with the stress
of the job required not only the support back at the
office but outlets to distract. From my mid-thirties
onwards, as I travelled, the visual and performing
arts were not only about enjoyment but, a bit like
canal boats, a respite from my professional life and
they became even more significant at The Bridge.
By now I was travelling abroad on a regular basis,
which gave me the opportunity to see performances I
would not otherwise have seen. For example, despite
not being keen on ballet, I had the chance to see the
Bolshoi dance Swan Lake inside the Kremlin and
even I could see how beautiful it was compared with
a very clunky performance at Sydney Opera House
a few years earlier. However, the latter performance
had the redeeming feature of two intervals in the
Opera House bar which looked out, through a
panoramic window, on to the harbour and because
it was a Saturday there was a large number of yachts
racing across the water. Ironically, there is a lot of
ballet music I really like.

Having said that, the visual arts scene was alive
and well. Over the years I have watched with
fascination the exciting development of the visual
arts in Australia including Aborigine painting and
sculpture which, whilst retaining the spirit of the past,

has embraced the media and methods of the present. The sadness for me was that so often exciting, talented artists were never seen in the Northern hemisphere mainly because, wrongly, Australia was viewed by the art establishment in the UK as an artistic desert. However, finally, an exhibition of contemporary Australian art arrived in the UK in 2013 with a show at the Royal Academy.

In December 1997 a group of friends and colleagues successfully launched a shared canal boat called Concorde. The group of ten included four with social work backgrounds, and others from public service organisations all of whom needed this refuge from professional life which continued for me until 2007, when Liz and I bought our own boat. As I write this twenty-one years later the remaining shareholders have just sold Concorde.

By the end of 1997 however, despite the supports available to me and the outlets within the arts, all the exposure to the horrors children were coping with and managing an organisation was catching up with me, and I worried that I could become a liability after 13 years within the organisation, my tiredness impeding development. I therefore told the Bridge Management Committee, now chaired by Marion Lowe (formerly Chief Executive of the National Foster Care Association) I intended to stand down as chief executive in December 1999 and hoped this would give them time to work out how they wanted to move forward.

To my great delight my deputy Renuka was selected to replace me. Renuka was someone you could be totally honest with, have a laugh with, or a good argument with, providing a working relationship with the same compassion for and commitment to children and young people. Renuka is incredibly bright with an extensive academic pedigree that I lacked and therefore added immeasurably to the work of the organisation.

Within a few months I experienced my first major health scare when I developed a deep vein thrombosis (DVT) though it went unrecognised for six months, even whilst flying around Europe as President of the European Forum for Child Welfare, an organisation that represented all of the major child care charities and NGOs across the continent. In August 2000 I flew to Sydney for a conference and a short holiday. I climbed Sydney Harbour Bridge before flying home. When I eventually saw a consultant, he asked me to go through my travel activities in the previous six months and by the time I got to Sydney his face went white! Surgery followed and an immediate resignation from EFCW.

I continued to undertake some work for The Bridge but by 2005 I knew it was time to go for good. To make sure I really did retire I ended my registration as a social worker so that I would not be tempted back to professional practice but of course my experiences cannot be erased.

I did get involved in something that could be classed as work. In the late 90s I set up a separate trading company for The Bridge to run its publishing services to produce research reports, Inquiry Reports and books. This separated out the publishing tasks from the everyday work and was more efficient of time and skills. However, in 2002 the organisation decided it no longer wanted to continue with this arrangement and rather than see it close Liz and I took it over and looked after all Bridge publications including successfully experimenting with a digital series of research papers. In addition, we took on work from other fields such as a fascinating book by a friend, Ann Spencer, that was an account of a cycle ride from Land's End to John O'Groats in her sixties, called *Pedalling a Dream* (37).

Full of humour, pensioner angst and achievement, it sold well enough to cover its costs.

Looking back, the questions I constantly ask myself are: "Did I learn from life's experience and did I and my colleagues make a difference?" I suspect the answer is yes and no in both instances.

There is no doubt I learnt a lot about myself. As a young man I was more likely to seek consensus and avoid conflict in relationships at all costs and defer to people who I perceived as being more knowledgeable, without necessarily exploring the accuracy of what I was being told, something which could lead to problems. But as the years went by the analytical approach which started to develop during my professional training became much more part of me, which in my personal life made others feel less comfortable and made me more difficult to live with but which, professionally, probably made me more effective.

This analytical approach developed rapidly in the wake of my unhappy experience at British Agencies for Adoption and Fostering and strengthened my resolve to ensure that when decisions needed to be taken they would be based on evidence not biased opinion, which is generally unreliable. It also made my determination to fight injustice much stronger.

But it was the analytical approach that led me away from religious faith because what I was seeing worked out in organised religion did not match the underlying principles (and I am not just talking about Christianity here) and far too often failed to care for the most vulnerable such as victims of child abuse, or discrimination against particular groups such as gay people or on grounds of race. Religion was also used by some as a cause of too much strife, from the Middle East to Northern Ireland and Africa or flying planes into buildings, sending young men and women into situations as suicide bombers or using a "religious war" as an excuse to justify rape and murder.

Then there is the attitude of Christian churches towards young single mothers well into the second half of the 20th century (and in some religions it is still an issue today) where children were taken away from them just because they were single and given (and in some cases sold) for adoption and, far worse, for sexual exploitation. Martin Sixsmith's book *The Lost Child of Philomena Lee* (38) describes the horror for mothers and children in Ireland, but it was not just in Ireland.

When I first came into social work in the 1960s, babies of single parents in the UK were also being taken away as a matter of routine just because the mother was single but using all kinds of spurious excuses. In addition, older children were removed by children's charities in the UK, at the behest of UK post-war governments, transported from residential care to former colonies where many were abused, neglected and refused the chance to return home.

They had been told their parents were dead when they were very much alive and looking for their children, a practice that went on until well into the 1960s. Or those religions/cultures that practise and justify female genital mutilation, or force young teenagers into abusive marriages all in the name of religion and culture or more accurately institutional politics. Or religious groups that welcome paedophiles on their release from prison because they "have got religion and repented", who are then allowed to have contact with children and start their activities all over again. Is all this naivety, stupidity, misogyny or wilfulness? Either way it seems to me to have little to do with religious faith.

It still goes on in other organisations, the recent spate of cases involving children being trafficked into prostitution from local authority care being a prime example, where for years senior managers failed to act as they should. As I write this the current Prime Minister has just asked the speaker of the House of Commons to set up a new procedure to deal with sexual harassment and assault by MPs to protect the reputation of Parliament. No Prime Minister, it should be about changing behaviour to protect the staff who work there.

Not all religious faiths and leadership are abusive or corrupt, far from it. Readers will have experience of many, many people in religious faiths, priests, nuns, ministers, rabbis, imams and lay people who will demonstrate extraordinary compassion and who feel as frustrated with their institutions when they behave badly as I do. Similarly, people of no faith also possess that same extraordinary compassion and feel the same frustrations when the leaderships of institutions they are involved with behave badly. The problem comes when bigots, or in the case of violence, thugs attach a cloak of respectability to their behaviour by attributing it to their so called religious beliefs or political causes.

Where religion is effective it seems to me is when it is driven by compassion. For example, nuns like Sister Philomena in Salford who was well aware of reality and would always go the "extra mile" to help women and children. Or the more visible work done by the late Anglican and Roman Catholic Bishops of Liverpool, David Sheppard (former England cricket captain and priest in Stepney) and Derek Worlock who, on behalf of the many unemployed in the city, took on Margaret Thatcher's government and the extreme left-wing council which between them were exacerbating a situation that caused even more poverty.

Others include the work done by St Martin in the

Fields with homeless people, which goes on year after year asking nothing in return from those benefiting from the service provided. The Muslim doctors and nurses trying, at great risk to themselves, to treat fighters and civilians from both sides of the civil war in Syria. Desmond Tutu who was as important as Nelson Mandela to the peaceful transition of South Africa from a country ruled by apartheid to the description of it as a "rainbow nation". Martin Luther King and the Civil Rights struggle in the USA.

I am sure readers will have their own examples. Although I do not pray, the following words reflect a simple prayer where compassion is right at the centre of its meaning:

> *To give and not to count the cost and*
> *Not to ask anything in return, not even belief.*

I am not anti-religion *per se* but find prejudice of every kind unacceptable and as the list above shows these great people made a difference through their compassion, concern for people from all backgrounds and their needs, including standing against injustice.

Compassion, however, is not the sole prerogative of religion. People who are not religious can show just as much compassion and do. Just think of the thousands of people who, not because of religious belief, work in the aid world or in hospitals or schools or act as volunteers giving services to the elderly or disabled people all over the world, very often alongside people who do have a religious faith. Imagine what our country and the wider world would be like without them.

Go back in history to a mixture of women of faith and no faith who, against the odds, but at great cost, made sure that the process leading to universal women's voting rights was achieved or women like the workers at Ford of Dagenham with a little help from Barbara Castle, who ensured that they no longer had to work for lower pay than men. Their efforts heralded an equal pay act that, whilst it is on the statute book, sadly has not achieved equality of pay for women in this country, yet! Helen Suzman in South Africa was a lone white anti-apartheid voice in the South African parliament who became a significant part of the civil rights struggle.

Closer to home there is MP Jess Phillips who is outspoken and articulate on women's issues, domestic abuse and, because she worked for many years in a refuge, can speak authoritatively and powerfully on these subjects as well as many others. Or Harriet Harman, one of the best leaders the Labour Party never had who has been a champion of women's rights throughout her career. Or what about the late Princess Diana (remember I am a Republican) who changed world governments' views on landmines by bravely walking through a field which had been mined. Yes, attempts had been made to clear the field but there is no guarantee that all the mines would be found. The Princess, by one action, changed the way the media, politicians and the public viewed HIV/ AIDS by sitting on a hospital bed holding the hand of a very ill AIDS victim. A troubled soul, possibly, but compassionate, passionate about the charities she supported, and brave.

Or two very different young women Chelsea Clinton and Devi Sridhar who are using their academic settings and skills to try to improve the way world health systems are managed by governments so that where there are major problems occurring in the developing world they can be addressed much faster, thereby saving thousands of lives (39). Or the youngest and brave Nobel Peace Prize winner Malala Yousafzai whose story is a world phenomenon. Or JK

Rowling, who having written the extraordinary Harry Potter book series, has used her influence and her new wealth to set up a Foundation focusing on preventing children, in areas of natural or man-made disasters, from being put into dubious institutions, trafficked or worse and where no effort is made to find their families, who may be searching for them.

Add today all the brave women who are coming forward to report sexual assaults and harassment and being pilloried for their efforts. It is often suggested that men are apparently confused and no longer know where the sexual boundaries are. I have known men who were sexual predators and they knew perfectly well that their behaviour was unacceptable to society and where the boundaries were but believed they could get away with it because they believed that they were entitled to have whatever they wanted. Similarly, the perennial sex pest within an office or factory or a community always knew they were over stepping the boundaries, not only believed they could get away with it but that women enjoyed the so called "banter". In reality it was about the men concerned using their power against women, exemplified by the disgraceful video clip of Donald Trump not only boasting about groping women but that somehow that was what they wanted.

Did my colleagues and I make a difference professionally? Probably yes and no. We made a difference, with one or two exceptions, when we were working to prevent the suffering of children. Yes, we made a difference in those inquiries where managers and staff worked closely with us because together we changed the immediate practice, or where managers and professionals elsewhere individually picked up and understood the lessons we were trying to communicate.

Probably, knowledge of neglect was enhanced

because of the Paul Inquiry but on the other big lessons; sharing information and the integrated systems needed for this; understanding the concept of dangerousness; or achieving long term therapy services for children who had been abused, then the answer to my question is still a work in progress. Changing cultures that have been in existence across many agencies for decades requires more than I or my colleagues were capable of influencing sufficiently.

Perhaps others may feel they can view what we achieved or did not achieve more objectively and take a more optimistic or pessimistic view of the work we undertook, or it might need a greater time distance from events before an accurate judgement can be made.

Into Retirement

Retirement might suggest a life of ease to many, and it's true that my time is now much more my own, but a working life dedicated to effecting change of the most profound kind, exposed to the worst of human behaviour has meant that, while I retired from the day-to-day pressures of work, retirement from the need to contribute, the need to make a difference, the need to expose injustice or bad management and worse, is impossible. By allowing people to get away with these things, by adopting a policy of wilful blindness, a phenomenon eloquently highlighted by Margaret Heffernan in her book *Wilful Blindness* (40), we allow bad things to happen.

However, attempting to decide what to do with retirement is a strange decision to face. Do you carry on doing more of the same or something different, and if the latter what? Are there skills I can transfer? Like so much of my life a whole collection of things emerged around a similar time, I got married again and moved to mid-Wales, where I anticipated spending more time on our canal boat, especially as Liz loved the canals as much as I do and over the years I had developed a deep love of the arts.

So, what to do? Certainly, spending more time on our canal boat Betty B is not difficult, exploring sections of the country that cannot be seen any other way, with a mixture of beautiful countryside, wildlife and our industrial heritage, which provided a wonderful refuge from work, enabling "batteries to be recharged" and it's even better in retirement because we can spend several months every summer almost living in a "bubble".

When Liz and I moved to Glasbury-on-Wye this was a completely new part of the country to both of us. For those who have never heard of Glasbury it is a village in Wales in the county of Powys, four miles from the book town of Hay-on-Wye. It is stunningly beautiful, situated as it is on either bank of the River Wye, nestling under the peaks of the Black Mountains and with extraordinary light and skies. So, it is hardly surprising that so many artists of various kinds live here; fifteen in Glasbury alone at the last count! I think of it as the centre of the universe but no doubt there will be those who disagree.

After fifteen years I look back on a privileged life working with friends and colleagues in building a very active community arts organisation, called Glasbury Arts. It has brought some amazing performers and artists into the area. People like internationally renowned violinists Rachel Podger and Tasmin Little, international jazz diva Jacqui Dankworth and Catrin Finch, now acknowledged as the world's greatest living harpist. That recital would never have happened if a local fifteen-year-old young woman, Fran Hughes, had not asked me whether Glasbury

Arts could invite Catrin to appear in the village. Then Fran was rather perplexed when I said, "who is Catrin Finch" and she had to explain. I heard what she had to say and Catrin came to Glasbury eighteen months later.

But the origins of Glasbury Arts are located in our visual arts exhibition which has brought wonderful internationally acknowledged Welsh painters and sculptors such as Martyn Jones, Charles Burton, Alan Salisbury, Brendan Burns and Sally Mathews to this annual event. It has a unique place in the Welsh arts calendar by bringing together some of Wales's best artists with local talent including students from our local secondary school. In addition, the organisation has a very strong partnership with Cyfarthfa Castle Museum and Gallery in Merthyr Tydfil (one of Wales's hidden gems), thanks to the help of Gareth Davies, the former chair of the Contemporary Arts Society for Wales, who introduced me to their brilliant curator and general manager, Kelly Powell. In 2017 this culminated in Glasbury Arts co-curating, with the Castle (and the Redhouse), a "Celebration of Welsh Contemporary Painting" featuring the artists listed above plus others such as Kate Freeman, Gus Payne, John Darlison, and Shani Rhys James. We hoped it would succeed sufficiently to become a bi-annual event and Kelly Powell and the rest of us on the planning group are now planning the 2019 event with five galleries.

All of this led to an annual education programme including ceramics and painting courses. In addition, inspired by Catrin Finch, Glasbury Arts launched, and organises annually, a harp summer school, the only one in Wales. The harp is the iconic national instrument of Wales, a tradition that needs nurturing, and the school has some very exciting tutors, including Katherine Thomas, Harriet Earis, Gwenan Gibbard,

Eleanor Turner, Adriano Sangineto and Lily Neil. In addition, one of our former students, Martha Powell, now in music college, has come back as an assistant tutor to work alongside Catrin Meek.

Neither has literature been forgotten, thanks to the talented Jenny Valentine, living in the village writing superb novels for a teenage audience who started running young people's writing workshops for us in 2007. Her first novel, *Finding Violet Park* (40), had been very well received and, just before the first workshop was due to take place, Jenny received the Guardian 2007 award for Children's Fiction. Jenny has continued to work with us whenever she can. Now we also have regular digital workshops for young people covering animation and film making with Nick Brown.

The development of the organisation has been based on a very strong volunteer base, many of whom have been with us from the beginning. People like Alyson Hearn, Caitriona Cartwright, Dawn Cripps. Suzy Wildee, Kayleigh Hughes, Ian Foster, Julie Dawson, Mike Harding, Juliet Parker Smith, Iona De Winton, Hannah Lee, Annie Berry, Kathy Ricketts, Darren Ricketts, Geraldine Cleary, Geraldine Done, Jean and Peter Powell and of course Liz plus many, many more. Others have reached a stage of life where they can no longer physically offer to volunteer but each one has found other ways to show their support.

One of the highlights of the development of Glasbury Arts has been the involvement of so many young people from Gwernyfed High School. We have been very grateful to our patrons, Lord David and Lady Margaret Lipsey, Jeffrey Babb, and Catrin Finch for their long-term support. In addition, the Welsh Assembly Government Cabinet Secretary for

Education and our local Assembly Member, Kirsty Williams has lent us her support from our very hesitant beginning in 2003 and enthusiastically continues to do so. Last but not least the long-term publicity service has enthusiastically and very professionally been provided by Philippa May.

This is a long way from child abuse and child death. It has brought me into a new world which provides enjoyment, inspiration and concentrates on constructive educational development for people of all ages. The continuing development of Glasbury Arts is a story all of its own with community values at its central core.

Retirement also brought a chance to further develop my interest in photography, which now, thanks to the inspiration of abstract painter Kate Freeman, has taken me into an exploration of abstract photography and this too is another story in its own right.

What I did not expect in retirement was to use my investigative and analytical skills from my professional career in working with others in an ongoing battle with Powys Education Department which was, and still is, one of the most financially and managerially challenged local authorities in Wales and like a giant tanker will take a very long time to turn around.

For years there had been serious problems in terms of schools' deficits, particularly in secondary schools. In 2012 a friend of mine, Bill Johnson, and I started investigating the problem of school deficits with judicious use of the Freedom of Information legislation. What we found was truly shocking given secondary schools in Powys are small compared to their counterparts in urban areas. We produced a detailed paper (41) and as a result the Office of the Auditor General for Wales investigated the situation at Brecon High School and how it was managed by the local authority, confirming our findings. The report, which was scathing, was never shared by senior officers with the local authority cabinet.

Published in 2013, our report (41) showed there were five secondary schools with unauthorised, and therefore unlawful, deficits totalling over £1.8m, including Brecon High School's £705,000. Instead of dealing with the problem, all kinds of "fixes" were used. For example, the Powys cabinet authorised a "special gift of £120,000" to Brecon High School to offset against their budget deficit. The reader may ask why? We did. The explanation given was as compensation for the local authority not being supportive enough. Can you imagine your bank, when looking at your unapproved overdraft, saying, "have another £10,000 as we did not support you enough to stop you over spending"? No, neither can I.

If that was not bad enough, £150,000 disappeared out of the deficit of the same school and when I have challenged this, as I have done on a regular basis, I was told it was a cut. When I asked which cuts, I have never received an answer. This meant the school's deficit was reduced overnight from £705,000 to £435,000 and, to compound the stupidity, the cabinet converted the deficit to a loan so that the school no longer had a deficit. The current Education Portfolio Holder recently admitted it was a mistake, whilst a senior officer in a meeting with a colleague, Punch Maughan and myself, described it more accurately as a "fiddle". Actually it was illegal. Bill Johnson, Punch Maughan and myself are part of a small group called "Powys Education Reform Movement "(PERM), which is trying to work with the local authority and others to bring about change. Whether we succeed remains to be seen.

By 2016 the Auditor General for Wales, following up another referral from me, had identified eight out of twelve secondary schools with unlawful deficits, but Powys County Council argued it would be five by the end of the financial year, which was accepted by the auditors (42). However, six months later the number was up to nine and still the local authority failed to use its statutory powers to rein in the deficits. There are two other secondary schools with licensed (and lawful) deficits but the total schools deficit (including those before 2014) in secondary schools is now heading upwards of £4m, leaving just one secondary school, Gwernyfed High School in surplus.

Instead of dealing with the problem, the local authority's idea of saving money included trying to close our high achieving local secondary school, Gwernyfed High School (the only one with a financial surplus) four times in eight years, in a misguided attempt to save the Brecon school which, on the last occasion in 2016, was in special measures and had a deficit heading towards £1.6 million with just 500 pupils. The authority backed down but two years down the line we have learned that the cost to Powys County Council Education Department of trying to close our school was £1m, which could have been spent on education. From the point of view of our school it was money well spent because the local authority was forced to set up a statutory consultation process (something they did not usually bother with) and it became clear they could not win, but the situation should never have arisen.

There was a time just after we had moved to the

area when Gwernyfed High School went through a very bad period in terms of the quality of education and had a proposal been made to close it, thwarting the local authority would have been difficult and I would have not got involved. However, now the school has some of the best academic results in Powys and Wales and runs a surplus which it has done for ten years.

Today it is designated by the Welsh Government as one of its twelve pioneer schools, the deputy head of the arts faculty has been appointed an arts and creative ambassador jointly by the Welsh Government and Arts Council Wales, the Institute of Physics designated the science teacher as one of six teachers of the year in 2016. Significantly, Gwernyfed also has thirty-five community organisations working within the school and playing an important part in the life of the school. In other words, not a school to close.

Just for good measure the Welsh Assembly Government has a policy and strategy (unlike that in England) to improve creatively across all schools and subjects and our local secondary school is central to achieving implementation. So innovatory is the policy, the OECD is encouraging education policy makers across the world to visit Wales to see for themselves the innovations being put in place.

The two most impressive features about the fight to keep the school open was the way the superb head teacher John Williams and all the staff worked so hard to ensure that, whatever was going on around them, students stayed on track with their education and parents, the community and community councils all came together to support the school.

For me, when Powys attempted to close our local secondary school, the plan had too many uncomfortable echoes of life in my last secondary school where I watched a very good school disappear before my eyes because of local government stupidity, with devastating results for me. Whilst I have played a small part, along with a number of others, in trying to sort out the local authority's deficit problems and ensuring our good secondary school continued, it was one of life's privileges and this too is another story and one that has yet to be completed.

However, I have a warning for the Powys Education Department. If they fail to sort the problems out or secure the future of our local secondary school before I die I will return to haunt every county councillor day in day out and, if necessary, I will bring together a community of spirits, including people like Charles Dickens and Dr Barnardo, to join in and make life very difficult. If the local authority thinks I have been too harsh up to now, me coming back as an active ghost will be much worse. They have been warned!

Chapter 9 - Epilogue

Do not go gentle into that good night,
Old age should burn and rave at close of day;
Rage, rage against the dying of the light.
Dylan Thomas

Time to reflect on where I have got to. What to call myself? I am not a social worker or a young man so how about *recycled man?* The term came from a man who used to run a green-grocer's shop in Hay-on-Wye, retired, and sometimes runs a market stall and described himself as recycled, which is a great way of viewing retirement. Some would, however, describe me as a grumpy old man. It is true I am much more impatient with people, particularly if I think they are wasting my time. I am at a stage of life when my own history is far longer than my future can ever be and as I do not know how much time I have left, I object to other people wasting what I see as my precious time.

What sets off my recycled grumpiness? All sorts of things, such as being patronised because someone looks at me and sees an old person and calls me love or dear or offers to help me count out my change when shopping because they think I cannot cope. Being invisible to such an extent that middle aged, and it has to be said, middle class people, both men and women, barge me out of a queue.

Listening to the *Today* programme gets my blood pressure up, not just because of the incessant inhumanity between people in so many walks of life but the pompous jargon. Following the dreadful neglect of patients at a Staffordshire hospital, the national inspection service had been strengthened and there was an interview on the programme with the new head of the service who kept saying they were going for "a deep dive", a phrase he repeated in every sentence, but the interviewer failed to ask for a definition. Eventually I worked out he was talking about a much more intensive inspection regime, so why not say so instead of talking about "deep dive"?

My life has been littered with this sort of nonsense, remember "pushing the envelope", how do you do that and where do you push it to? What about "a menu of options" or "crossing the Rubicon" or "a raft of measures" or "rolling out programmes going forward" or "drilling down into the issues"? Would it not be dreadful if the man deep diving got in the way of the guy drilling down, could be a nasty accident? In January 2014 an interview, again on the *Today* programme, elicited the two following unbelievable pieces of jargon: *fetishization of kitchens and fetishization of cooking*, what does that mean? Has Ann Summers taken over B&Q and Waitrose? What's wrong with plain English? I do not condemn jargon outright, because different professions need to find new technical terms to define or explain developing theoretical issues. What I object to is its use to try to make the speaker look clever or confuse the public. More recently I become irate when interviewees on a radio or television programme are asked a question and start their answer with a one-word sentence. "So". Except it sounds more like "Soo". Makes no sense.

Then there is the political mantra beloved of policy makers, senior executives and politicians "we are learning the lessons" to which I referred earlier, said with exaggerated sincerity so that you know nothing will change because by the time the next disaster comes around they will have long gone and another bunch will be making the same claim but, oh yes, on fabulously high salaries.

Just to see what would happen I took those jargonistic phrases that make my blood boil and turned them into a sentence as follows:

> *Soo. Today I pushed the envelope from a menu of options, by thinking outside of the box, selecting the fetishization of kitchens and cooking as a priority in order to roll out my programme going forward with a full raft of measures which included a deep dive that meant I also had to drill down into the issues just before I crossed the Rubicon to learn lessons in the round.*

That clear?

Bankers though are my real bête noir, especially if they then go into politics. When the banking crisis hit in 2008, it was the greed of some bankers that caused the virtual destruction of a pension that I had spent 42 years paying into, whilst the senior bankers who were part of the problem walked away with millions of pounds in severance and pension payments. That was bad enough, but their replacements were awarded "golden hellos" and excessive bonuses so as to "incentivise" them to get out of bed in the morning. It beggars belief that professionals, so called, being paid the size of salary they earn, need so much more. If banks want to give extra money to incentivise people, try paying bonuses to those on the lowest pay. The government's austerity mantra for the last ten years has been *"we are all in this together"*, unless you are an overpaid bank executive, or a member of the UK Government that is.

Unfortunately, it's not just bankers; what about the BBC? This is supposed to be a public service organisation, but it pays ridiculous fees, salaries and bonuses. Then it emerged that the broadcaster had one of the largest gender pay gaps in public service organisations. Then there was an abject failure to stop young people being molested and then trying to cover it up. Do the words public service not mean to serve the public?

Then there is avoidance of corporation tax by major companies, Amazon et al. Need I say more?

However, the thing that riles me more than anything else is injustice. Looking at our world today my Mum and Dad must be turning in their graves (or in their case, their urns) as our Home Office have attempted to return (illegally to Caribbean countries) hundreds of adults (now in their sixties and seventies) who came here as children with their parents by invitation to help re-build our shattered country in the 1940s and 50s. They have become known as the Windrush Generation after the name of the ship that brought the first group to this country.

These are people who have lived and worked here all their adult life and paid their taxes. Albert Thompson (not his real name) was told in November 2017 by the Royal Marsden Hospital that he was not eligible for radiotherapy for his cancer on the NHS because it was thought he was not in Britain legally, despite having worked here all his life, paid taxes and had a national insurance and NHS number. He then lost his job and was evicted from his council flat. Or Leighton Joseph Robinson, who went to Jamaica for his birthday for the first time since he came to Britain, but when he tried to return he was refused entry because he only had a Jamaican passport. It took twenty-one months for him to return but only after the intervention of a solicitor in Wales. That, however, was not the end of the story. On his return he had lost his job, was prosecuted for non-payment of rent and evicted from his council flat.

Once the problem was identified the government carried on regardless until a dramatic U-turn in the face of overwhelming media pressure and public disquiet. The U-turn was chaotic, with the Home Secretary blaming civil servants, the Prime Minister blaming the Labour Party and Labour blaming the Tory Party and ultimately the Home Secretary having to resign. The blame game was because they all realised that, whoever was responsible, the Home Office actions were carried out in a racist and reprehensible way and no one wanted to be tarred with that brush.

As I write this, the revelations on this subject keep coming. For example a document published by the Guardian newspaper, from the former Home Secretary Amber Rudd to the Prime Minister (and former Home Secretary) Theresa May dated 30th January 2018. With public pressure already building, the Home Secretary tells the Prime Minister in her memo she intends to give immigration greater *"teeth"* to hunt down illegal immigrants and accelerate Britain's deportation programme. This new stance builds on Theresa May's policy as Home Secretary to make Britain a *"hostile environment for illegal immigrants"*. The memo adds the Home Secretary sets out *"her ambitious plans to increase removals, arresting, detaining and forcibly removing immigrants and ruthlessly prioritising resources to the programme including transferring funding from fighting crime."* It has also just been announced that 63 members of the "Windrush Generation" have been, as British citizens, *illegally* deported to the

Caribbean, whilst others who just went on holiday to their homeland for the first time for half a century, were refused re-entry to the UK.

Ultimately it is Theresa May's government that has implemented this awful policy thereby bringing about the recommendations Enoch Powell made fifty years ago in his "Rivers of Blood" speech in Smethwick that all immigrants should go home. What gets lost in all this is that Labour in 1948 passed an act making it possible for people from the Commonwealth (or Empire as it was then) to come here as UK citizens. But it was Sir Winston Churchill and Enoch Powell who signed a letter in 1951 to Caribbean governments inviting their citizens to come to the UK to help re-build our war-torn country with full rights. In case the reader is puzzled about the signatories to that letter, the Tories had just won an election and Enoch Powell was the minister responsible for immigration. That's right; the same Enoch Powell who would 15 years later go on to make his infamous "Rivers of Blood" speech. Yet here we are sixty-seven years further on with a Tory Government wanting to deport those same people who came here legally and by invitation of a Tory Government. If only politicians would learn their own history.

Let me be clear, whatever the intentions, the action was racist and brings shame on our country. We now know there are many people from all parts of the world facing similar actions and the government is dragging its feet in putting things right.

Sadly, it's not just on the political right these problems exist, the Labour party has been both slow and clumsy in dealing with anti-Semitism. Even in the face of many Labour MPs standing up in the House of Commons in a Conservative debate, describing the horrible and unacceptable behaviour directed at them by Labour members, the Leader of the Opposition failed dismally to deal with the bigots in the party's ranks. It's not that we cannot criticise the Israeli Government when they behave badly towards minorities like the Palestinians but rather we should not stereotype or insult people just because of their heritage. We now find ourselves in the situation where the Leader of the Labour Party, like Theresa May for the Tories, completely fails to understand or act to deal with this racism. A complete lack of leadership, and unforgiveable.

The political parties also contain people who behave as though they hate Palestinians, Muslims, gay people, those with disabilities or who are just poor. It's all tied up in dreadful racism, discrimination and injustice towards anyone who is different. All parties must not only say that they do not tolerate injustice and discrimination but demonstrate it by clear actions such as kicking out those who think nothing of distressing many people by their dreadful words and actions. Theresa May in 1997 described her party as the "Nasty Party" but she will end up, with help of the Leader of Her Majesty's opposition, unless they act, presiding over the development of the UK into the "nasty society". The one glimmer of hope is that the British public as usual are way ahead of the government. Polls on the question of what has become known as the "Windrush generation" are showing that seventy percent of the British public are opposed to their deportation and loss of civil rights.

Just as I am about to send this manuscript to my editor for a final edit it has been revealed that the Home Office has deported 17 professionals, teachers, doctors, nurses and lawyers under the anti-terrorism legislation, none of whom have shown any sign of such activity, and a further 1000 are awaiting deportation under the same legislation and again without any sign or evidence of guilt. Why? How are we going to replace them? They were here legally but because they all made very minor errors in their eighty-page application for citizenship (one inaccurately wrote down their income, it was out by £1.20), the Home Office, illegally, tried to make out they were terrorists. It has again just been announced that the policy is being reviewed, something that should not have been necessary.

Look closely at education, children's services, social care within local authorities or the increasing levels of people living on lower incomes or poverty or who are homeless, and the crisis in the NHS, the story is frighteningly similar. Over the last ten years the UK government cuts, plus those by local authorities, despite all their protestations, have targeted the most vulnerable in our society. Then the popular media and right-wing politicians denigrate the homeless as feckless, people who go to food banks in order to survive became scroungers, and adults who report historical abuse are described as only being after financial compensation.

This last issue is raised whenever the need for each new historical abuse investigation opens up. Recently, a senior football official, commenting on a number of adults who were reporting abuse, racist, physical or sexual, by football coaches ruining their lives and careers, questioned why they had not reported the abuse earlier and went on to say he "smelled the whiff of money" e.g. compensation. He was unable to comprehend the fear or trauma they experienced, as so many had across the sporting spectrum and indulged in denial, which foolish people have done from the Holocaust right up to the present. Denial, more than anything else, is the biggest barrier to preventing awful things happening to vulnerable people. It does not matter where we live, abuse, whether it be about race or physical or sexual maltreatment of children or women, exists and individuals pretending it is not there has the effect of preventing a secure future for those people.

Whilst all this is happening, politicians in the cabinet have been publicly quarrelling over a soft or hard Brexit when it is clear they do not have a halfway decent plan between them. The Prime Minister who is so weak she had to persuade the Democratic Unionist Party to support her in return for a £1.5 billion "sweetener" for Northern Ireland, who then threatened to "crash the car" in the middle of negotiations. Whether the Prime Minister and her cabinet will still be in post when this book is published remains an open question.

The Labour Party may not have the responsibility for the Brexit negotiations, but they are making a poor show of opposing the government. Up until the referendum their leader was a Brexit leaver but now he is somewhere between leave and remain, or is he?

If all these irresponsible politicians put as much energy and money in to solving our health and social problems as they expended on Brexit we would not be having a winter crisis in the NHS, we would not be leaving so many cancer diagnoses until it's too late, our schools would not be asking parents to buy books or equipment or not filling teacher vacancies, not providing high quality vocational education for those young people who cannot go to university, elderly and frail people would not be left isolated or not knowing whether there is a bed for them, or children at risk of abuse being left in dangerous situations.

Last winter in the midst of the NHS winter crisis, when my wife Liz had to undergo surgery for cancer and I had to wait nearly a year for cataract surgery, we were able to observe close-up the difficulties being faced by staff. Whilst in hospital I noticed the ward Liz was in was one of a suite of four, but three were empty. I asked how it was that there were three empty wards when we are repeatedly told by politicians and the media that the NHS problems are caused by a shortage of beds because us oldies are bed blocking? The answer was there was no shortage of beds but an acute shortage of nursing staff and doctors.

Since the Brexit referendum there has been a mass exodus of European staff as they no longer felt secure or welcome here because the government was using them as negotiating pawns, whilst existing British staff were becoming demoralised and leaving to work for agencies who hire them back to the NHS at double the price. In addition, there was a cap on recruitment of new staff from outside the EU and training for homegrown staff cannot keep up with the need. I am writing this in June 2018 and the government has just acknowledged that we need 35,000 nurses and nearly 10,000 doctors to plug the gap. That is what Brexit has already achieved and we are still in the EU. Whatever readers' views are, for or against Brexit, I do not believe voters intended to vote for the destruction of these services, any one of which we all may need now or in the future.

Both of us were so impressed at the wonderful care we received from consultants, registrars, hospital nurses, GPs, community and district nurses and, in my case, a local optician. All not only went the extra mile but a long way further. When there was a threat of my eye surgery being cancelled for a fourth time because of incompetence by the senior non-medical managers, the entire clinical team, knowing of Liz's condition, pulled out all the stops to make sure I was not cancelled again, irrespective of what senior managers thought. We could not have asked for more. If only the senior managers with their fat cat salaries and bonuses, could match the dedication of the clinical and nursing staff.

Finally, the government has recognised that there should be no cap on doctors and nurses coming here and ending the deportation of law abiding health staff. Too little, too late. Now the Government has announced, under more pressure, an annual 3.4 percent increase in NHS expenditure, still leaving the UK lagging behind the rest of major European countries who are also increasing their spending on health, and behind their preventive and early diagnostic services, that we need. Some of that 3.4 percent is supposedly coming from a saving from leaving the EU but given we are heading for a transition period running through to December 2020 and a further back stop period the country will still have to make a financial contribution to Europe throughout those periods, so where is the saving? The Prime Minister also announced that there would be tax rises to help pay for the extra expenditure, but who will they fall on? Governments tend to place a greater tax burden on the lowest paid, allowing high earners to get away scot free – will it be any different this time?

What is needed is for health, social care, children's services and education to be removed from government and party political control and placed in an external NOT FOR PROFIT system with joined-up processes and robust regulation, run by people who understand those services, as opposed to managers who have not a clue what the services are about.

Which brings me to Grenfell Tower, a fire that should never have happened. The surviving residents have been treated very badly by the local authority and the government. The thing that most symbolically sums up the contempt shown to survivors is the fact that Theresa May went very quickly to the scene of the fire but failed to meet survivors. I cannot think of a single Prime Minister, however good or bad they were, who would have failed to understand that the need to meet the people mattered most. Jeremy Corbyn got there, Blair, Major, Thatcher, Wilson would have got there but not Theresa May. Now go back to the blitz in 1940. Winston Churchill was clambering over bomb damaged streets to meet survivors several times a week, the King and Queen doing the same. It has taken twelve months for the Prime Minister to acknowledge that she made a mistake and regrets not meeting the survivors a year ago but said it did not indicate she did not care. What else did it indicate?

Just for good measure it has just been announced that the Home Office has told the adult children of an immigrant who died in the Grenfell fire that they will not issue a visa until they can prove they need to be here. Our current government is clearly aiming to be the meanest and most disgraceful since the second world war, where the words callous and cruel define what it stands for. In such a febrile atmosphere, can we or the politicians be surprised that the immigration service would look for soft targets in order to do their political masters' bidding, but the plan has backfired, and the policy has caused immense suffering which will continue.

It explains why I have not joined a political party. Instead at each election I look hard at the integrity, compassion, honesty and care for people that each candidate demonstrates (or not) before deciding how to vote. How my poor Mum and Dad would have hated all these different ways of discriminating against people. My parents are not here now and so, for as long as I live, I will go on calling all the injustices I have listed in this memoir for what they are – a mixture of utter bigotry, racism, misogyny, wide ranging discrimination and callousness.

However, recycled man should not be just about having a rant, because life has much more to offer than grumbling. Just look around and see the good things that are there. For example, travel, whether it is for a day, a week, a month, or even longer, in this country or abroad should open our eyes to new experiences, stretch our intellectual view of the world and its people and should make us better human beings.

As I have said I am fortunate to live in the beautiful scenery around Glasbury-on-Wye with a backcloth of the Black Mountains, a view of the Brecon Beacons to the west, one of the most beautiful rivers in the country, the Wye, meandering through our village landscape and no traffic lights because the traffic is so light. It comes as a shock when you drive to the nearest big town. Then there is our local restaurant, the River Café Glasbury, which serves up great food and a warm welcome in equal measures and has also been a great supporter of Glasbury Arts, as have other local companies like WH Ricketts and Sons, Hereford and Brecon Windows.

Where I live is not just about beautiful scenery but is a place with people where I feel I can belong. It's also a place where young people care about their community, want to socialise with the older generation, who, when they see you standing on a bus offer up their seat, who are polite and courteous when you walk through the local secondary school

(Gwernyfed), who can put together a planetarium night for the whole community to enjoy, who routinely produce stunning art work and who make you smile because of who they are.

It's a place where people volunteer to contribute to their community from running a village hall or providing community transport but ask nothing in return. Glasbury and its surrounding villages are in a rural area with people of all ages and backgrounds volunteering to meet so many needs. If they stopped, the villages would be the poorer.

Then there are friends and acquaintances that run like a thread through your life over decades and give you riches more valuable than money. They are people who care about you even when you do not realise or when you do not treat them as well as you might. They make the world go around.

What about those magic moments with family that are so much a part of my life, such as watching children growing up and starting their journey towards recycled-land. My life has been full of such moments with my daughter and her husband, my son and my grandchildren and without them my existence would be much the poorer. Family life is not always straightforward, and we cannot always agree. For example, my daughter is an Anglican priest, and whilst I cannot share her religious beliefs, I am so impressed with the way she has translated her faith into compassion and commitment for the people she serves. The moments we spend as father and daughter are so precious. Mairion married a really nice, caring man who, together with my grandchildren, Sophie, Owen and Rhys are never far from my thoughts. Similarly, my grown-up son has not had an easy life because of dyslexia, but we have shared times which might seem unimportant to others but to me are so significant. He is a very good photographer, whose concern for people less fortunate than himself is expansive. As I write this he has just announced he is getting married to Jenny. Last but by no means least, my wife Liz who puts up with this strange old guy.

Being part of a career that gave me an opportunity to contribute to or be part of the world around me, even if it was only in a small way. That was a privilege which added to the quality of my life but with it came responsibility. It led on to being part of the development of an arts organisation that provided another privileged opportunity I could not have envisaged.

Do I have regrets? Yes of course, but not many. Primarily they are about unintended hurt and distress I have caused. However, when I look back over my seventy-six years the thing that amazes me most is just how many wonderful people played a significant part in my life that would have been so much poorer without them. I have been so lucky to meet so many inspiring people in everyday life and for me this is almost the most important part of my story. Those mentioned in this book are only a small representation of a much wider experience, because without those links to other warm, caring human beings what is there left?

Am I positive about the future? Yes! I have faith in the young people in our society and their ability to bring positive change. For years people have said young people do not care about the lives of other people, which is not my experience, or that they did not care about the democratic process. If it were true, could we blame them as they have been disenfranchised by succeeding generations and, in the case of university students, forced into huge debt.

However, the young people I meet are full of compassion and determination to change things for the better. The 2017 election demonstrated that young people are interested in the democratic process, coming out in their thousands to vote and contributing to an electoral upset. In other words, they saw they could make a difference, but we will never know how, only others will be able to judge.

Many of the young people I meet are inspirational, bright and determined, characteristics they will need if they are to improve a world old fogies like me are leaving behind. Far too often I hear people of my generation complaining about young people, which says more about the complainers than the younger generation. To all those complainers I say move over, it is a world of young people now and people like me need to be supportive of and inspired by their efforts, because we are the past.

Can I still have aims to work towards? Of course! I want to go on as long as I can, supporting community arts, making it possible for people of all ages to participate, whatever their circumstance. I want to go on championing education in a way that makes it a positive, creative and enriching experience for students of all ages. I want to go on pushing local education authorities, such as Powys, so that they get on board with the Welsh Government's Creative education strategy to give our young people a head start. Education in today's world is the key to a young person's future and I want every young person to have equal opportunities to make the most of their life. I want to continue to push local education authorities to manage their finances in a way that is both effective and lawful.

Whether we make a difference will depend on

the choices we make, to sit on the edge and remain uninvolved or move into the middle to try to contribute, or to call out injustice whether it be racism, anti-Semitism, misogyny or anything else. This sentiment has been put far more eloquently, originally attributed to Edmund Burke, and explains why sitting on the edge is not an option:

"All it takes for evil to triumph is for good men (people) to do nothing".

We all need to rage on.

References

1. Professor Antony King, Ivor Crewe – *Blunders of our Governments* – One World Publications – 2013

2. *British Nationality Act* – HMSO – 1948

3. *Abortion Act* – HMSO – 1967

4. John Fitzgerald – *Understanding Disruption* – British Agencies for Adoption and Fostering – 1983 and 1990

5. *Be My Parent* – Adoption Resource Exchange – 1980

6. Bill and Brenda Mercer, John Fitzgerald – *Building New Families Through Adoption and Fostering* – Basil Blackwell's – 1982

7. Jane Rowe – *Children Who Wait* – Association of Adoption and Fostering – 1973

8. Celia Borland, Maureen Thom – *Bruce's Story* – Children's Society – 1986, 1987, 1989

9. Anne Jeffery, Debbie Malone – *Needs Game* – Berkshire Social Services and The Bridge Child Care Development Service – 1992

10. *Sukina Report* – The Bridge Child Development Service – 1991

11. *Paul Report* – The Bridge Child Development Service – 1995

12.   AH Clausen, PM Crittenden – *Physical and Psychological Maltreatment: relations among types of maltreatment in child abuse and neglect* – Pergamon Press (USA) 1991

13.   D Rosenberg, H Cantwell – *Consequences of Neglect, Individual and Societal* – Bailliere and Tindall – 1993

14.   D Skuse – *Emotional Abuse and Neglect, ABC of Child Abuse* – BMJ Publishing – 1994

15.   *Part 8 Case Review Overview Report into deaths of Heather and Charmaine West and related murders* – Gloucestershire Area Child Protection Committee – 1995

16.   Sir Ronald Waterhouse – *Lost In Care* – HMSO - 1999

17.   Ed, John Fitzgerald, Mary Jean Pritchard – *Brenton's Story* – Children's Society – 1996

18.   Sarah Jones, Emma Davidson – *My Life in Words and Pictures* – The Bridge Child Care Development Service – 1994

19.   John Fitzgerald – *Child Protection and the Computer Age* – The Bridge Child Care Consultancy Service – 1999

20.   Lord Laming – *The Victoria Climbié Inquiry Report* – HMSO – 2003

21.   A Hagel – *Dangerous Care: Reviewing the risks to children from their carers* – Policy Studies Institute and The Bridge Child Care Development Service – 1998

22. Renuka Jeyarajah Dent – BridgeALERT: Key information for Identifying Children in Danger plus Training Pack – The Bridge Child Care Development Service – 1998

23. Renuka Jeyarajah Dent – *Dangerous Care: Working to Protect Children* – The Bridge Child Care Development Service – 1998

24. *Childhood Lost* – The Bridge Child Care Development Service – 2001

25. *Daniel Pelka Serious Case Review* – Coventry Safeguarding Board – 2013

26. *UN CONVENTION OF THE RIGHTS OF THE CHILD – UNITED NATIONS – 1989*

27. Professor E Munro CBE – *Avoidable and unavoidable mistakes in child protection work* – British Journal of Social work – 1996.

28. Irving L. Janis – *Victims of Groupthink* – JOURNAL ARTICLE – *Political Psychology* – Vol. 12, No. 2), pp. 247-278 – International Society of Political Psychology – June 1912

29. Professor E Munro CBE – *Munro review of child protection: final report – a Child-centered system* – Department of Education – 2011

30. *Care of Children Committee Report (known as Curtis Committee Report)* – HMSO – 1946

31. *Committee of Inquiry into the Care and Supervision Provided in Relation to Maria Colwell, Report – HMSO – 1974*

32. *A child in Trust, The report of the inquiry into the case of Jasmine Beckford* – HMSO – 1986

33. *Rikki Neave Part Case Review Report* – Bridge Child Care Development Service – 1994

34. Stephen Sedley QC – *A Litany of Excuses: Lessons from Death of Tyra Henry* – Department of Health – 1988

35. Sir William Utting – *People like Us* – HMSO – 1997

36. Ann Spencer – *Peddling a Dream* – Cwm Consultation and Publishing Service Ltd – 2005

37. M Sixsmith – *Lost Child of Philomena* – Pan Macmillan – 2010

38. Margaret Heffernan – *Wilful Blindness: Why We Ignore the Obvious* – Walker & Company – 2012

39. Chelsea Clinton and Devi Sridhar – *Governing Global Health* – Oxford University Press – 2017

40. Jenny Valentine – *Finding Violet Park* – Harper and Collins – 2007

41. Updated Review of Five Schools with Largest Deficits for Period September 2008 to March 2012 – January 2013

42. Office of Auditor General – Report of Review of Powys Education Department Financial Management – June 2017